THE POWER OF

you

For further information:

The Kabbalah Centre
155 E. 48th St., New York, NY 10017
1062 S. Robertson Blvd., Los Angeles, CA 90035

1.800.Kabbalah
www.kabbalah.com

First Edition, November 2004
Printed in USA
ISBN 1-57189-247-8

Design: Hyun Min Lee

THE POWER OF
you

Kabbalistic wisdom to create the movie of your life

www.kabbalah.com™

KABBALIST RAV P.S. BERG

DEDICATION

May the Light of Binah, that has guided the Rav and Karen to be the beacons of Light for us all, overflow abundantly throughout humanity, encircling the world with blessing, miracles, wonders, clarity, healing, protection, love and unity and may It shine upon our magical children Yonatan and Rivka, in all Its glory.

—Yosef and Miriam

CONTENTS

ACKNOWLEDGMENTS

For my wife, Karen. In the vastness of cosmic space and the infinity of lifetimes, it is my bliss to be your soul mate and to share a lifetime with you.

INTRODUCTION

In the 20th century and in the first years of the 21st, so much has been accomplished by science and technology. A book much longer than this one would be needed to enumerate the many advances, both material and intellectual, that I have seen in my lifetime. Unfortunately, this undeniable progress has been accompanied by a directly proportional increase in emotional pain, stress-related illness, and plain old unhappiness.

Can anything be done about this? Is there a way to bring our inner experience of life up to speed with the material abundance that surrounds us? Can we close the gap between what we see with our eyes and what we feel in our hearts?

The answer to these questions is an emphatic Yes! And in the chapters that follow, you will learn how to implement that Yes! through the tools and teachings of Kabbalah, the world's oldest body of spiritual wisdom.

But even as I write these words, I'm aware of certain ideas that are often associated with the application of ancient traditions to contemporary life.

You might anticipate, for example, that you'll be pointed in the direction of detachment, transcendence, and noninvolvement with everyday concerns.

You might expect that Kabbalah will urge you to free yourself from desire, to be content with what you have, and to ponder the meaning of "less is more."

In general, you might suspect that "timeless wisdom" will translate into "old"—and that this oldness, while perhaps having an appeal when you're in a contemplative mood, will ultimately be of marginal benefit to your daily life.

At the outset, I want to emphasize that none of these preconceptions has any relevance to Kabbalah. To the contrary, Kabbalah is about intense engagement with everyday life. Kabbalah brings fulfillment of your most authentic desires, not escape from them.

In these pages, I intend to bring you the authentic teachings of Kabbalah in the context of the modern world. As you'll learn, the movie that is your life may be a comedy, a tragedy, a melodrama, or a farce—but the choice is yours. What's more, the ability to change your movie is always in your hands. Indeed, this is the essential "Power of You."

"FOR ALL WHO HAVE A DESIRE TO LEARN . . ."

It was in the early 1970s that my wife, Karen, and I first undertook to bring the wisdom of Kabbalah to all who had a desire to learn. This was a revolutionary idea. For centuries, it had been said that grave dangers threatened anyone who ventured into this area of knowledge; in any given generation, only an elite group of scholars could safely learn Kabbalah. These warnings had done their work well. The ancient teachings had indeed remained hidden, and there was good reason for this. The spiritual level of humankind was not yet ready for Kabbalah. But there came a time when Karen and I realized that things were beginning to change. We therefore opened Kabbalah Centre locations around the world, and we were soon gaining the assistance of loving souls who shared our desire to disseminate Kabbalah's sacred wisdom.

What is the essence of this wisdom? Kabbalah teaches that there are only two basic concepts that we must know in order to remove chaos from our lives. Kabbalists refer to the first of these concepts as Restriction and the second as the Desire to Receive for the Purpose of Sharing. In the end, of course, these two ideas resolve into one. As Rav Hillel put it, "Love your neighbor as yourself. Everything else is commentary."

It should be added, however, that commentary which comprises the great texts and teachings of the sages is by no means unimportant! For it is from these sources that we come to know the true whys and hows of creation, thereby gaining freedom from humanity's abundant misconceptions. Of these misconceptions, among the most prevalent and damaging is that of a Supreme Being who dispenses rewards and punishments.

Unfortunately, the image of this Supreme Being is deeply rooted in human consciousness, and much time and effort will be required to erase it. Nonetheless, Kabbalah teaches that all our experiences—past, present, and future—are the result of our own thoughts and actions, and nothing else.

Of course, the distinction between thought and action was a major point of contention in the scientific world until the revolutionary breakthroughs of 20th century physics. Until this time, the mind was described as separate from the body. Disease, for example, was understood as an essentially physical malfunction that was in no way connected to the processes of the mind and heart. Yet the very word dis-ease points the way to a true understanding of health and illness—that is to say, that stress and disease are one and the same. Webster's defines ease as "freedom from pain, worry, trouble, or strain." The prefix dis means "the opposite of." Consequently, and perhaps without intending to do so, the medical profession accurately defined illness as a condition in which freedom from pain, worry, trouble, or strain is replaced by physical and psychic chaos.

Most people are not aware that our current problems are perpetuated by the narrow base from which we search for solutions. Rather than ask why these problems exist at the most fundamental level, we focus on "the tip of the iceberg." Moving beyond this framework will require a profound revolution in consciousness. Of course, even people who recognize this necessity are frightened by it; they're frightened of having to alter their "lifestyles." Yet lifestyle is not the level of our being that Kabbalah addresses. Instead, the kabbalist strives for a truly basic change in human consciousness.

By making the study of Kabbalah available to the world through this book and through all our work, The Kabbalah Centre intends not only to assist individuals in achieving altered states of consciousness, but also to help them create their own security shields, with which they can protect themselves from a hostile and chaotic environment. Specific objectives of our work include the development and expansion of humanity's overall frame of reference and, on an individual level, freedom from ever needing to resort to expressions such as "lucky" or "unlucky."

COSMIC AWARENESS

From a kabbalistic standpoint, the secret to taking control of our lives resides in our awareness of the cosmos, which is the primary factor influencing everything we experience. This is not to say that our thoughts, our emotions, and the state of our mental and physical health do not affect the outcome of our lives and the way in which we live them. However, they are not the primary source of the positive or negative energies that evolve into our everyday experience of the world.

Simply put, we have lost control of what happens to us because we are not aware of the true causes. Kabbalah changes that. Kabbalah is a body of spiritual teachings and tools that empowers individual human beings to control their destinies. Kabbalah teaches us that there are no mysteries. Life is not a case of one person being lucky while another is not. This knowledge affords us the opportunity to tap the awesome power of the cosmos, to redirect our life movie, and even to reshoot scenes as necessary to avert the secondary influences that wreak havoc on our civilization and create chaos and disorder in our lives.

We are now at that moment in human existence which kabbalistic Astrology identifies as the Age of Aquarius. Here an entirely new reality awaits us. But first, the very existence of this reality must enter our consciousness.

As I write these words and chapters, my first task will thus be to raise your state of awareness so that you may participate fully in the Age of Aquarius. There is really nothing complex about this. It's simply a matter of seeing the world—the contemporary world in which we all live—as it really is.

The Power of You presents the kabbalistic perspective on the ills that beset our society. This perspective reveals the fact that individual human beings create their own unique energy fields of contentment or lack thereof. In other words, you make your own movie. Yet in order for you to make a movie you want to see—not to mention act in—you must first withdraw your attention from the notion that "somebody up there doesn't like me."

If your life seems to be a negative environment, you must take responsibility for it. You must become aware that you have caused these manifestations and their influence over you. Even more important, just as the stresses and negative circumstances that plague humanity originate within humanity's own energy fields, so too must you understand that the solutions to these problems will emerge only from your own individual efforts.

The dismal track record of "outside intervention"—be it chemical, psychiatric, surgical, or all of the above—testifies to the validity of this precept. *The Power of You* shows how to regain the essential right of self-determination. It vividly depicts how to change reactive, robotic behavior into an experience of conscious, self-controlled progress toward fulfillment.

CHAPTER ONE:

THE POWER OF THE COSMOS

THE REAL GOAL

Again and again, books on personal development and success emphasize the importance of setting well-defined goals. Readers are urged to make lists of their goals, to read those lists every day, and even to tape them to the bathroom mirror and in other strategic locations around the house. I'm sure many people take this advice to heart, perhaps writing down their desire for a new car or an exciting career. In all probability, however, very few people indicate their desire for one of the most valuable and elusive of all possible goals. The goal to which I am referring is peace of mind—and nothing is harder to come by in the modern world.

Why is peace of mind so difficult to attain? Let me be very clear about this: Our hearts and minds are under constant attack from the cosmos, and inner tranquillity is hardly compatible with this state of warfare. This continuous bombardment of thoughts— thoughts that seem random but are almost uniformly negative in character—is relentless. If we try to relax after a difficult day, we are not permitted the luxury of a quiet mind. This bombardment continues when we try to fall asleep, and it's still going on when we get out of bed in the morning.

Ending this assault for even a few moments is for most people a truly monumental task. After a while, the vast majority of individuals merely resign themselves to a constant state of disquiet. The battle is simply too furious to keep waging, and there's no relief in sight.

Amid all this turbulence, the really surprising fact is that most people experience the bombardment of negativity as something that originates from within themselves. Until we recognize the extent to which we are subjected to it, however, we can hardly begin to improve our sense of well-being.

Kabbalah can answer many of our questions about the cosmic influences that permeate our waking lives and that disturb our sleep as well. We may ask, for instance, whether the cosmos influences and affects all people in the same way. And if not, why not? In response, the kabbalists tell us very clearly that we are all influenced by astral energies in different ways. What, then, determines how and why each individual is touched by the cosmic powers in a particular manner? What factors force us to think and behave in ways that later cause us to look back and ask ourselves, "Why did I do that?" or "How could such a thought have ever entered my mind?"

To deal with these questions, let's invoke the movie metaphor once again. Kabbalah teaches us that reincarnation—the movie of prior lifetimes—is responsible for who we are, what we do, and how we feel. Our creativity, our emotions, and our intelligence are scripted into this film, which is constantly replaying itself in one remake or another. The production of these remakes has an intelligence of its own. On the basis of our innumerable past actions, both positive and negative, we create a new version of the same movie—and the process by which this takes place is intimately connected to the lineup of astral bodies at the time of our birth.

In short, we get what we ask for—and we must begin to ask for something radically different in our lives. For until we do so, the cosmic attack will only continue and intensify. An entire social and cultural transformation is necessary, but this can take place only at the individual level, one person at a time. In the Age of Aquarius, we can no longer depend on government intervention or any other agency or authority to extricate us from our present condition. In essence, the problem is you, and the only way to solve it is through The Power of You.

THE MECHANICS OF THE POWER OF YOU

How does The Power of You operate? The human nervous system and the brain are a system of infinite complexity that remains deeply mysterious in many ways. The mind, for example, has the ability to translate information from the remote past as well as to focus attention on the distant future. Indeed, it is these characteristics that distinguish people from other animals. As human beings, we are inherently drawn to the cosmos. Why? Because the cosmos contains the necessary ingredients for human fulfillment. Furthermore, the cosmos is concerned with sharing its beneficence even more strongly than we desire to receive it. As it is written, "More than the calf wants to suckle, the cow wants to be milked."

Intermingled with this intrinsic desire to share, however, the cosmos also contains negative energy-intelligence. As an interface, the cosmos communicates our past lives with a full complement of negative and positive activity. In our interactions with our environment, there is a continuous interplay between the celestial cosmic world and our experience of reality. More specifically, every human being consists of two realities: the positive reality of the soul, and the negative reality that comprises our five senses and our physical bodies. Bear in mind, however, that negativity is not the same as evil. Negativity is simply the energy force that we must work through and overcome in order to connect with the higher dimension. The shape of our lives depends on which of the two realities dominates our consciousness.

Regarding the causes of negative events in our lives, it's important to be aware of the kabbalistic concept of "Evil Eye." This concept refers simply to the care we should take to avoid attracting the attention of negative forces. As Rav Shimon Bar Yohai remarked, people possessed of an Evil Eye carry with them the destroying negative force, as a result of which other people must be on their guard and not come near them. A biblical example of a man with an Evil Eye was Balaam, of whom it is written, "Thus saith the man whose eye is closed." Balaam was a channel of negative energy, and the negative force was drawn wherever he fixed his gaze. Knowing this, Balaam sought to fix his sight on the nation of Israel so that he might destroy everything he looked upon.

Although Balaam searched for a vulnerable point toward which he could direct his cosmic attack, his efforts were to no avail. The people of Israel themselves controlled the negative energy-intelligence transmitted by the cosmos. As a result, Balaam's ability to channel this enormous power of devastation was stopped dead in its tracks. The people of Israel were not vulnerable because they had created a security shield with which they could stave off an attack. Those who are without such a shield, however, can become victims both of the Evil Eye and of other negative cosmic influences.

BEYOND SPACE AND TIME

According to *The Zohar*, a day is near when the long-hidden secrets of nature will at last be revealed. This knowledge will afford us access to the domain that lies beyond space and time. It will provide us with a framework for understanding not only the observable universe, but also that which lies beyond the range of observation in the metaphysical realm. In the everyday world, we have no trouble identifying material reality. It has body and substance; we can see it and touch it. But if we explore the foundations of what we perceive as solid, physical reality, we find that the basic building blocks of nature are something else entirely. Subatomic particles do not even occupy specific locations in space and time. The fundamental properties upon which the material world is constructed are in fact illusions. The only certainty is the thought, the energy-intelligence, that we are sharing from moment to moment.

The renowned British physicist Sir James Jeans summed this up when he wrote, "The universe was looking more like a big thought than a big machine." Here the kabbalist and the physicist are in complete accord, particularly with regard to the presence of physical pain and disease. Modern physics would have us believe that there is no reality other than thought. To its thinking, physicality itself is not a foundation but merely a distraction. Our environment of illness and suffering is recognized as a distortion. Physicality is significant mainly for the way in which it interferes with our thought processes, often completely obscuring them.

This interference is the power of the Desire to Receive for Oneself Alone, which can be identified as material intelligence. By contrast, the energy-intelligence of the spirit is known as the Desire to Receive for the Purpose of Sharing. The former is the material force that creates havoc in the universe. Kabbalistic teachings emphasize this as the fundamental and essential cause of chaos in our lives.

A SECURITY SHIELD AGAINST VULNERABILITY

The Zohar tells us that the lack of a security shield is the foundation of all misfortune. Yet with proper and accurate knowledge both of Kabbalah and of cosmology, we can rise above the influence of the stars and cosmic negative influences. For most of us, concerted effort and focused attention on the cosmic danger zones represent the first security measures against the array of misfortunes that currently assail humanity. When judgment is rendered as payment for past negative activity, we must be prepared for that judgment to express itself through the negative energies that are already present in our own minds and bodies. If internal security shields are not in place, we are left vulnerable to stress, disease, and misfortune of all kinds. Ultimately, however, we have no one to blame but ourselves.

How can we know when a judgment is about to be rendered? We must be on guard whenever we come upon an opportunity to commit an immoral deed, an act closely connected to a Desire to Receive for Oneself Alone. If at that moment we fail in the *Tikkune* process—that is, the karmic correction that takes place over many lifetimes—we create in ourselves a void in which the Creator has no presence. We then become vulnerable to an assault by the negativity that exists in the cosmos, and there is no telling what form that attack will take.

Remember that this attack is possible only because of the inner void from which the beneficence of the Creator has been excluded. When this beneficence is absent, room is created for the Desire to Receive for Oneself Alone to become manifest. "Like attracts like" is a spiritual law of the universe. Darkness attracts darkness; Creator attracts Creator. The Desire to Receive for the Self Alone is darkness, and therefore it will attract negativity. But the Desire to Receive for the Purpose of Sharing reveals the unity with the Creator that is our true essence. This eliminates vulnerability and confers security and protection.

Vulnerability of any kind cannot be seen as a consequence of "bad luck." Quantum theory has taught us to see the universe as a web of thoughts and interactions strung together among the parts of a unified whole. The most important element of the kabbalistic worldview is its awareness of the unity that underlies all events. In contrast to this, the negative side's vision of the universe is one of fragmentation and destruction. Which vision will prevail in the life of a given individual? The answer depends on our own actions and consciousness.

NATURAL DISASTERS

With regard to this discussion of vulnerability, I feel compelled to raise the subject of natural disasters as they are perceived through the eyes of the kabbalist. Some would argue that this subject should best be left alone lest we incur the wrath of religionists who declare that "the Lord, in His mysterious ways, knows and has His reasons for raining destruction upon various parts of our globe." But does the Creator really play dice with the world's inhabitants?

Earthquakes and other disasters are often called "acts of God"— but this implies that our ability to deter or delay such incidents, or even prevent them from taking place, is not even worthy of mention. We are simply victims. We are vulnerable, and there is nothing we can do about it.

In thinking about this, it's important to remember something that is repeatedly stated in *The Zohar*: "That which is below is above, and that which is above is below." This principle allows us to reveal the connection between what takes place in the most distant galaxies, in the subatomic realm far beneath the power of our perception, and in the physical world as we experience it in our everyday lives.

The Zohar continues:

> Rav Isaac once drew near to a mountain, and there beheld a man sleeping under a tree. He sat down. Suddenly and without warning the earth began to quake

violently and became full of fissures. The tree was uproot-
ed and fell to the ground. The earth was rising and falling.

And the man beneath it woke and wept and lamented
with mourning and sounds of sorrow. For at this
moment a great supernal minister is now being
appointed in Heaven, who will cause terrible misfortune to the world. This quaking of the earth is meant
as a portent and warning to you. At this Rav Isaac felt
a trembling and said: Verily it is written, For three
things the earth quakes. For a servant when he
reigneth. For an odious woman when she is married,
and a handmaid who is heir to her mistress.

As *The Zohar* reveals, earthquakes are a manifestation of the fall
of kings, queens, and political leaders and their replacement by
representatives of the negative side. The power of negativity is
greatly enhanced by the desire to receive for ourselves alone,
and the result is expressed through natural disasters. In other
words, our own actions, and even our thoughts and feelings,
determine the behavior of our surroundings.

Geological fault lines, therefore, are not the primary factor
underlying earthquakes. Rather, earthquakes are the inevitable
consequence of negative human behavior. Were self-serving
activities transformed first into the restriction of ego-based
desire and second into the desire to receive in order to share,
fault lines would no longer threaten the California coast, and
Las Vegas would no longer live in fear of becoming the new
western border of the United States!

In fact, the entire worldview of our culture should be carefully reexamined. Galileo proposed that true scientists should restrict their studies to the essential properties of physical entities. In his view, only factors that could be measured and precisely quantified were worthy of consideration. Subjective experiences—such as smell, taste, hearing, or sight—were to be excluded from the province of science. But by directing our attention to quantifiable properties alone, we lose touch with the 99 percent of reality that completely surrounds and envelops us. And while Werner Heisenberg's uncertainty principle has been assimilated into the most advanced levels of scientific thought for at least 50 years, the layperson has remained unaware of the important role of the self and its perceptions in all forms of scientific endeavor.

ACTS OF GOD: WE BEAR SOLE RESPONSIBILITY

The basic tenets of Kabbalah have always taught that we bear sole responsibility for what happens to us and to our environment. We and we alone—and not any machine—have been given awesome power to influence the entire planet and the cosmos. This idea is strikingly revealed by *The Zohar* in considering the biblical narration of the Great Flood: "And the Lord saw the earth and behold it was corrupt; for all humanity had corrupted their way upon the earth."

How can the earth become corrupt? Is the earth governed by the rules of reward and punishment? The answer is this: Since man governs and influences the earth, his behavior and actions, if they are evil, imbue their evil spirit within the land. When humanity commits sin upon sin, openly and flagrantly, the earth behaves accordingly. This includes all the so-called natural disasters.

Earthquakes, floods, tornadoes, and hurricanes are the "natural" result of man's evil inclination and behavior. Of course, once we have identified man as the underlying cause of such disasters, it follows that man can alter these events or even prevent them from happening in the first place. Yet the vast majority of humanity does not know or reflect upon what keeps the world—or themselves—together.

When the Creator brought the world into being, He made the heavens of fire (negative energy, which Kabbalah calls the Left Column) and water (positive energy, or what Kabbalah refers to as the Right Column). These elements were mingled together and were not put in harmony with each other. Only later were they brought together as one unified whole by the balancing power of the Central Column.

When the power of the Central Column is removed, however, the elements of creation quiver and shake, and the world trembles. As it is written, "Who shaketh the earth out of her place and the pillars thereof tremble." But when the force of the Central Column is activated, the world is supported by the three columns and thus remains in a balanced state.

In summary, *The Zohar* makes it perfectly clear that what have always been considered "acts of God" are in fact a corruption of the creative process. Natural disasters are of our own making. We have the power to stop these phenomena and prevent them from taking place. And if the world around us is all that evil, we—like Noah before us—can take matters into our own hands for the safety of ourselves and of our families. Noah was taught how to construct a security shield that would insulate him from the devastation brought on by the Great Flood. The Ark was a symbol and manifestation of the all-powerful force by which the flood waters were kept at bay. While everything around Noah perished, he remained alive.

Let this be a lesson for our generation, which has been exposed to so many "natural" and man-made disasters. We should not just hope and pray each day that we will be counted among the "lucky ones" or among the survivors. We can and must do something about it. Specifically, we must use the tools and teachings of Kabbalah to ensure that our thoughts and actions connect us to the forces of positivity as well as to the balance of the Central Column.

ADDICTIVE BEHAVIORS

According to the outdated, materialist view of the world, nature is no more than a machine operating outside the realm of humanity's participation. In the 17th century, Johannes Kepler devised empirical laws concerning planetary motion by studying astronomical tables. Galileo performed experiments to discover the laws of falling bodies. Then Isaac Newton described the universal laws of gravitation. In the 20th century, however, scientists suddenly uncovered a serious challenge to their ability to understand the universe. In their struggle to grasp the new reality of subatomic physics, they became painfully aware that their basic understanding of nature, as well as their fundamental ways of thinking, were inadequate to the task of describing the foundations of our natural environment. The average person, however, has not yet been compelled to face these uncomfortable facts.

As a result, masses of people have been programmed to believe that the extrapolation of the laws and principles of our universe is the purview of science and government—not a project suited to the individual. In other words, it is their view that this is a task that lies beyond The Power of You. If our present attitude is one of helplessness and hopelessness, it is because we as individuals have not seen or understood our own true power and significance. Consequently, we have not found a reason to take responsibility for our actions.

Perhaps we may find ourselves saying, "What difference does it really make whether I understand the universe, the world, or even the environment of my own city block? I know there are serious environmental problems, but I'm sure science will take care of them without any help from me!" This is a widespread way of thinking—a feeling of helplessness, combined with the questionable assumption that those in "authority" will take care of everything.

The vast majority of people, we have been led to believe, are incapable of intervening in the universe on anything beyond a very small scale, so they should simply not bother to do so. Yet there is proof all around us that those to whom we have entrusted our power have failed to create a society that is free of violence, suffering, pain, and widespread chaos.

THE POWER OF UNITY

In the boardroom of a multinational plastics manufacturer, a director of sales clicks his way through a series of exciting slides. Each slide depicts new products and packaging materials, all made of plastic. Soon humanity's food requirements will no longer need to be packaged in heavy, bulky paper receptacles or metal cans. New, lighter-than-air trays, bags, and bowls will provide an assortment of meals, from TV dinners to baby foods. In time, of course, the question will ultimately be asked, "Are any of these new plastics biodegradable?" Yet today, for the sake of expediency, questions pertaining to our future welfare and the welfare of this planet are deferred.

Given the desperate state of our environment, it has become abundantly clear that we can no longer afford the luxury of what I have termed "human myopia." We can no longer ignore the long-term effects that new technologies might have on our planet. Our myopia and shortsightedness have compelled us to live in a constant state of crisis management. The technologies we have created are severely disrupting the ecology of our planet's natural environment. The poisoning of our water supplies and the contamination of the air we breathe by toxic chemical waste pose grave threats to our very existence.

Enormous amounts of hazardous waste are the direct result of shortsightedness. Chemical companies have made repeated attempts to conceal the dangers of their manufacturing processes and waste hazards. As a result, the fabric of life that took generations to evolve is rapidly disappearing. When acid rain falls on our rivers, lakes, and oceans, it is absorbed by fish, plants, and other forms of life, thereby polluting the entire ecosystem—although the effects may not be felt for many years. Moreover, a number of severe nuclear accidents have already afflicted our planet. Major catastrophes such as Chernobyl either have taken their toll or have been narrowly averted. As human greed spurs the acceleration of nuclear accidents, we must ask, "How in the future are we to dispose of nuclear waste?" Each nuclear reactor annually produces tons of radioactive waste that remain toxic for thousands of years. People must become aware that no permanent, safe method for their disposal has yet been found.

The people or businesses responsible for these dangers feel no remorse or pain when they dump thousands of dangerous chemical compounds into our earth, rivers, and oceans. Human myopia prevents these irresponsible people from considering the problems they are creating for future generations as well as for their own offspring. From a kabbalistic standpoint, the problem with this reasoning is as follows: If indeed greed creates human myopia, then it is not only future generations such individuals have endangered but also themselves, as they will now become the victims of their own irresponsible actions by being reincarnated to the "scene of their crime." We must constantly be aware that our universe does not exist in a fragmented state, but rather has a unified direction. Evil actions are followed by consequences that affect the perpetrators of those actions. These perpetrators do not, in other words, get off scot-free. Rather, they suffer the consequences of their actions unless a correction is made either now or in future lifetimes. The kabbalistic world-view, along with its teachings and doctrines, can promote a people's information revolution that will inevitably force and create change—and this change must be nothing short of a cultural revolution.

I adopt this bleak outlook on the state of our health and physical well-being for two reasons. first, because we now stand at the brink of a global environmental breakdown. Hazards have reached such epic proportions that neither medicine nor government intervention can ensure a healthy society. Second, we must acknowledge that despite the many ominous warnings that have been issued about our future health and unsafe environment, there is still a state of balance that exists within the cosmos. Illness and negative human behavior, from a kabbalistic perspective, are not an isolated process. When we tap into the negativity that exists in the cosmos, the result is illness and disharmony. The nature of all things is seen as either in balance and in harmony with the cosmos or, conversely, in a state of disharmony with the fundamental principles of a dynamic cosmic reality.

In order to apply our study of the kabbalistic model to the development of a quantum holistic approach to universal interconnectedness and interdependence, we must first deal with two questions. We are looking for a "whole" approach in our life patterns, and in this framework we must ask, "To what extent is the kabbalistic view holistic? Which of its aspects can be adapt-ed to our cultural environment and surroundings?"

From a kabbalistic perspective, everything leads to one conclu-sion. This is the metaphysical quantum reality, the essence of which is "Love Thy Neighbor As Thyself." Break down the false distinction between what's best for you and what's best for the human beings and physical environment around you. When humanity achieves this shift in understanding, the entire uni-verse—both seen and unseen—will be revealed as a single unified whole.

SCIENCE AND THE BUSINESS WORLD

The influence of business has brought a disturbing imbalance to every facet of scientific endeavor. Just as the petrochemical companies have convinced the agricultural industry that our soil needs massive amounts of chemicals, so too have corpora-tions persuaded the medical establishment that in order to achieve good health, patients must undergo continuous drug treatments.

But I did not write this book to deride the business world, the scientific community, or the medical profession. Instead, my intention here is twofold.

first, I want to raise the consciousness of humanity to encom-pass an awareness of what is going on in our midst. If we are to believe the statistics of the cancer, heart, arthritis, and other foundations, it would appear that most Americans do not enjoy perfect or even satisfactory health. And even if there are some who still claim that things are just fine, we are reminded each day of the many other threats that prevent us from living safely in our homes or from walking our streets free of concern over assault by addicts or terrorists.

Second, I want to make humanity aware of the timeless system that Rav Shimon Bar Yohai introduced in *The Zohar*, and that is fully discussed in Rav Isaac Luria's *Gates of Meditation* and *Gate of the Holy Spirit*. These works provide us with the tools with which to obtain total and complete control of our inner space, though everything outside of us may be crumbling.

Richard Feynman, the renowned theoretical physicist, raised the following question in an address to undergraduates at the California Institute of Technology: "What do we mean by understanding something?" Feynman's grasp of human limitations, plus the recognition that we use only five percent of our mental power, led him to the following conclusion:

> We imagine that this complicated array of moving things which constitutes "the world" is something like a great chess game being played by the gods, and we are observers of the game. We do not know what the rules of the game are; all we are allowed to do is to watch. If we watch long enough, we may eventually catch on to a few of the rules. The rules of the game are what we mean by fundamental physics. Even if we know every rule, however, what we really can explain in terms of those rules is very limited, because almost

all situations are so enormously complicated that we cannot follow the plays of the game using the rules, much less tell what is going to happen next. We must, therefore, limit ourselves to the more basic question of the rules of the game. If we know the rules, we consider that we understand the world.

WATER: "TAKE THY ROD AND STRETCH OUT THY HAND . . ."

Given the environmental pollution that afflicts our world, it sounds like a bizarre science fiction story to claim that people acquainted with kabbalistic doctrines can and will enjoy fresh, uncontaminated water while people all around them seek fresh water with not a drop to be found. But Kabbalah does not consider this claim to lie beyond the humanity's grasp.

The Bible reads, "Take thy rod and stretch out thy hand upon the waters of Egypt, upon their streams, upon their rivers . . . that they become blood." And in turn *The Zohar* asks, "How was this possible? Could one rod be stretched over the entire country of Egypt, in which all the waters turned to blood?"

The explanation is this: The reference is to the River Nile, and to the fact that Aaron needed only to smite that river in order for all the other waters to be affected. What becomes quite evident is the quantum effect of Aaron and his spiritual consciousness. Aaron's dominion over the vast expanse of the cosmos was demonstrated when all the waters of Egypt became contaminated by blood. It was not necessary for Aaron to come in direct contact with each of the Egyptian rivers.

Let us now examine another phenomenon presented in *The Zohar*. The firmament in which the sun, moon, stars, and signs of the zodiac are suspended is the location in which the energy-intelligence of water resides, and from which the earth receives rain. The water is then dispersed and distributed far and wide. When negative energy-intelligences prevail over the universe, however, the lower, physical worlds do not nourish or tap the positive energy-intelligences of the upper firmament of the sun and moon.

The Zohar puts it this way: "The sword of the Creator is full of blood. Woe unto them who must drink from this Cup."

This brief phrase provides us with some notion of the profound difference between a superficial, conventional interpretation of the biblical text and its understanding as a cosmic code by the kabbalists. The energy-intelligence of each biblical verse has a bearing on the dynamic interplay of the universe. If the whole of the universe is thought of as an enormous, complex machine, then man is the technician who keeps the wheels of that machine turning by providing fuel at the appropriate time. The energy-intelligence of man's performance and activity is what essentially supplies this fuel. Consequently, man's presence is of central importance, since it unfolds against a background of cosmic infinity. The mystical conception of the Bible is fundamental to an understanding of the cosmos and its laws and principles. The Bible must be seen as a vast corpus symbolicum of the whole world. Out of this cosmic code of the reality of creation, the inexpressible mystery of the celestial realm emerges and becomes visible.

WATER AND NEGATIVITY

When humanity's negativity prevails within the cosmos, water turns into blood or another form of contamination. In other words, matter or material substance is subject to the dominion of the positive or negative energy-intelligences that are prevalent at any given time. The three fundamental forces of our universe—the Desire to Receive, the Desire to Share, and Restriction—are contained within an atom and are physically expressed and manifested in all material forms.

These three forces, designated in physics as the electron, the proton, and the neutron, portray the intrinsic thought energy-intelligences. The electron makes manifest the thought energy-intelligence of receiving, or the Left Column. The proton expresses the thought energy-intelligence of sharing, or the Right Column. The mysterious task of neutrons lies in the unification of the two opposing forces, proton and electron. In the kabbalistic view, the inherent characteristic of the neutron lies in the power of Restriction against desire to receive for the self alone.

The threat of pollution and contamination is the greatest danger facing humanity today. Yet our present crisis is the direct result of humanity's ability to invade the atomic structure. The

preponderance of negative human activity has created a dominion of negativity over the whole of the cosmos. Consequently,
pollution and contamination reflect this imbalance within the
universe. Water is influenced and controlled by a positive energy-intelligence, the proton.

Given the enormous negative human activity weaving itself
through every fabric of our lives, however, it is little wonder that
the forces of water's negative energy-intelligence now remain in
control of our food, our drink, and our global environment as a
whole.

The situation sometimes seems hopeless, without any relief in
sight. And were it not for kabbalistic knowledge, the future
ecology of our civilization might well remain in jeopardy and
the end of the earth might be a foreseeable reality. But for those
who follow the doctrines of Kabbalah, the future does not
appear as bleak as one might imagine.

The oft-quoted *Zohar* passage, "Woe unto those who will live at
that time [Age of Aquarius], yet happy those who will live at
that time," attests to a dual cosmic reality. Thus, there would
appear to be a cosmos within a cosmos. The teachings of
Kabbalah provide us with an opportunity to segregate ourselves
from the polluted physical cosmic reality and connect with the
unified all-embracing whole. The Lord, as Einstein remarked,
does not play dice with the universe. He is not a cruel, unsym-
pathetic producer, insensitive to the needs of humanity. Despite
our overwhelming global frustrations, we can do something
about our lives and our world!

THIS HAS HAPPENED BEFORE

A condition similar to what we face today—in which the entire world is dominated and controlled by negative forces—is described in the Bible, which refers to the period of the Exodus and the Middle Kingdom of Egypt. The idea of two cosmic realities is further elaborated on by *The Zohar*. The fate of Egypt was manifested in the waters of the Nile, and the punishment was inflicted from above and below. The people of Israel, connected with positive energy-intelligence, drank water. The Egyptians, drawn toward the negative energy, drank blood.

The separation of the universe's two realities is strikingly revealed by *The Zohar*'s interpretation of the Plague of Blood. The Israelites were in no way affected by the waters turning to blood. Moreover, the Israelites' control over water extended beyond their immediate environment. By virtue of the quantum effect, they made certain that water purchased from their fellow Israelites, once purified, remained in a pure state even when consumed by the Egyptians. This encouraging thought from the Biblical Code—and Kabbalah, the tool for deciphering that code—are precisely what will be necessary in our Age of Aquarius.

The summer of 1988, for example, was a revelation of things to come. The ocean was backing up. Medical waste began washing up on beaches from Long Island to the New Jersey coastline. Eventually the problem was brought under control—but in the effort to restore our oceans and farms, as in other struggles for a purer environment, we won the battle but lost the war. The moment one small victory is achieved, the forces of human greed and negativity are found to be at work against it.

Perhaps these early skirmishes over the environment will ultimately lead to a global consciousness and to an awareness of the fact that in the final analysis, all of humanity suffers from uncontrollable appetites. Perhaps this contamination and pollution will act as an impetus for all people to pull together against the common enemy—namely, greed and the Desire to Receive for Oneself Alone. Perhaps the shock that greed has engendered will mark a turnaround in our regard both for humankind and for all inhabitants of planet Earth.

The invasion of the marine environment by our persistent dumping of human toxins, radioactive waste, and chemicals is now returning to haunt us. There seems to be no escape from this reality. Within Kabbalah, however, lies Earth's salvation. As it is written in *The Zohar*:

> But they that are wise shall understand, for they are from the side of Binah (Intellegence), which is the Tree of Life. And because of these wise people it is written in Daniel, "And they that are wise shall shine as *The Zohar* (splendor) of the firmament; and they that are instrumental and responsible for turning the many to spiritual righteousness numbering as the stars for ever and ever." Only by virtue of your book, Rav Shimon Bar Yohai, which is the Book of Splendor (*Zohar*), will Israel taste from the Tree of Life, which is the Book of Splendor (*Zohar*). Only through the

instrument of *The Zohar* shall humanity be brought forth from exile with compassion!

With regard to the arrival of that day, *The Zohar* holds out more hope than does science, which must rely largely on randomness and probability. *The Zohar* can provide a direct link with the universal energy-intelligence and can present the world of metaphysics as an exact yet accessible science. Kabbalah holds answers to many of the most enigmatic aspects of nature, yet it remains elegantly simple.

The Zohar's view of our universe transcends the physical and occupies a frame that lies beyond space and time, whereas the modern age of physics remains fixed and limited to the view presented by Einstein. The kabbalistic vision of reality that we have described is based on an in-depth perception of the Bible's narration and tales.

Indeed, the descriptions provided by the Bible and *The Zohar* sound quite similar to those offered by modern cosmologists. These descriptions emphasize energy-intelligence systems strikingly similar to those that the kabbalists know as the Tree of Life:

> Rav Elazar said: The Lord will one day reestablish the world and strengthen the spirit of the sons of men so that they prolong their days forever. As it is written, "For as the days of a tree, so shall be the days of my people.

This is an allusion to Moses, through whom the Law was given and who bestowed life on men from the Tree of Life. And in truth, had Israel not sinned with the Golden Calf, they would have been proof against death, since the Tree of Life had been brought down to them.

THE PERSISTENCE OF PHYSICALITY

The primacy of physical appearance is a fact of everyday life that neither the scientist nor the kabbalist can ever escape. Both must always return from their laboratories or meditative states of consciousness to what has been referred to as the world of *botz* (mud).

For the present, this physicality maintains its grip by seldom, if ever, being the least bit altered by discoveries drawn from science or Kabbalah. The Surgeon General arms himself with laboratory tests warning against cigarette smoking, yet millions among us continue to smoke. The kabbalist returns from his meditation to offer the doctrine of Restriction in order to create positive effects both for the individual and for the world— yet millions continue to ignore him.

Why? Because we cannot differentiate that which is real from that which is illusion. The air we breathe has not taken on another appearance. The food we consume daily looks even better and shinier than before. Even the packaging has been improved. Water has for the most part retained its visible color and taste. Despite laboratory analysis, nothing has really changed. The

relentless search by modern science for the foundations underlying outward appearances has lent new validity to the belief
that physical appearances may well be a contrived illusion.

To be sure, we are now beginning to "read between the lines."
But there is nothing more between the lines than what we can
observe. We simply make use of expressions that we do not
examine seriously enough. Nevertheless, science is finally reaching a level of awakening. Even scientists now agree that we cannot consider physical reality anything more than illusory.

More specifically, scientists cannot offer a full description of
"reality" that can be demonstrated in the laboratory, nor can
they test "reality" effectively by technological means. It would
seem that manifest physical existence must dominate our thinking and behavior to the exclusion of the underlying nonphysi-
cal reality and causality.

The fundamental question is, "How shall we exist in two
worlds, the physical and metaphysical?" We must always be
aware that what we perceive on our mundane level should be in
conformity with the Desire to Receive for the Purpose of
Sharing. We must constantly take care that our daily actions are
in harmony with the aspects of sharing.

THE PRIMAL FORCE IS THE POWER OF YOU

We must always maintain awareness that our physical bodies are
composed of atoms, and that these atoms are 99% empty space.

And what are atoms if not energy-intelligence? Despite efforts by the scientific establishment to depict the power of the mind as playing no role in the workings of the cosmos, kabbalists continue to declare, Not so! Kabbalah has always taught that humanity is the central force in the cosmos. The Bible decreed that man surely could and would alter the influence of the cosmic order. The Creator recognized the necessity for a cosmos that allowed for the existence of the mind as a separate entity—a mind that could act on matter and cause it to behave in apparent violation of natural laws.

The Zohar declares that the Lord created two basic energy systems: one with a power of good and the other with an equivalent power of evil. These two fundamental systems could then exercise cosmic influence over man. It was then that the battle between good and evil began.

The idea of good and evil originated with the Tree of Knowledge of Good and Evil in the Book of Genesis. Humanity owes its corporeal existence to the sin of Adam. With the pollution of all physical matter derived from his connection to the Tree of Knowledge, Adam severed the connection between humanity and the Tree of Life. Before this time, the upper world and the earth's mundane existence were one thought, in perfect harmony. The wellsprings and channels through which everything in the higher celestial region flowed into the lower realms were still active, complete, and thoroughly compatible. All forms of corporeal existence were still perfectly attuned both with each other and with the Creator.

When Adam sinned, however, the cosmic connection was severed, and the order of things was turned into chaos. The energy was simply too hot to handle. Raw, naked energy of this intensity was not meant for our world. The Tree of Life thought process lay beyond the limits of time, space, and motion. The realm of the Tree of Knowledge of Good and Evil, with all its limiting factors, was insufficient to channel the heavenly communication. Consequently, the biblical text continues, ". . . they sewed fig leaves together and made for themselves garments." This was required to deal with the primal energy-intelligence that was now in force. It was not unlike the predicament of today's astronauts, who need space suits to protect them from the perils of radiation.

An individual soul retains its existence only in relation to its ability to sustain the energy-intelligence of the Creator. When Adam and Eve were abruptly distanced from the Creator by their sinful activity, they were no longer in accord with the dynamic interplay of the all-embracing whole. Their inability to handle the intensity of the Creator's presence left them naked. Humanity's own polluted, sinful behavior therefore underlies the crisis we face today.

Put more precisely, the division of the atom and all that has resulted from it is a scenario that was created by the sin of Adam. Man's every action is carried by the channels of the cosmos, whether we know it or not. Every earthquake, every supernova, every war that is waged is the direct result of violence and hatred emanating from the hearts of men. We have at our fingertips the ability to re-create Eden. Instead, however, we build nuclear warheads and prepare for war. Nations at war with each other wreak vengeance upon one another until they become exhausted and are destroyed. And even when the cloud of hatred has dissipated, the chaos and suffering of individual families remains. Humanity should long ago have recognized the futility of war and hatred, but envy and the Evil Eye stubbornly persist. Of course, pollution and contamination, along with all other manifestations of human negativity, can be removed through man's ability to change his ways and move toward a more positive approach. How? Through the teachings of Kabbalah in general—and in particular through *Restriction* (see chapter two) of ego-based desire and the power of sharing.

ENCIRCLING LIGHT: BEYOND THE OBSERVABLE WORLD

We have previously stated that Kabbalah provides the tools and teachings that can put us in touch with our soul consciousness. Let us now turn our attention to the all-encompassing form of energy-intelligence known as encircling Light.

The kabbalists tell us that no one who lives in the physical realm can come into direct contact with God. The immensity of the Creator's reality is simply too powerful. Kabbalah therefore speaks of "the Light" as levels of the Creator's energy that we can experience in the physical world. The more we fulfill our souls' potential, the more Light we will be able to reveal in our lives.

Encircling Light begins where soul consciousness ends and

extends beyond the soul consciousness of all humankind. Encircling Light is the all-pervasive consciousness of the universe, in which data from past, present, and future meet as one unified whole. For almost a century, physicists have informed us that our awareness perceives only a tiny fraction of what actually takes place around us. Even with the most powerful telescopes, we can see but a tiny portion of the universe; conversely, even the strongest electron microscope reveals only an infinitesimal fraction of the activity that takes place at the atomic level, and absolutely nothing of the subatomic realm. An apple would have to be expanded to the size of the earth before we could see even one of its atoms with the naked eye. And beneath that atomic dimension lies yet another world, the dimensions of which are many orders of magnitude smaller than even the most minuscule of atoms.

In the observable world—this tiny fraction of the immense spectrum of existence—we are hard pressed to find anything that bears even the faintest resemblance to fundamental truth. Indeed, the kabbalist will tell you that looking for truth in this world of illusion is like trying to find a subatomic particle in a haystack. In short, our five senses are notoriously unreliable judges of the world around us.

No doubt we have all been in situations in which a sound is heard, and every person in the room believes that sound came from a different direction. The sense of taste and the closely related sense of smell can easily be fooled by chemical scents and additives. Nor is our sense of touch any better at gauging reality; any number of fraternity pranks involving a blindfold, an ice cube, and the suggestion of fire can prove this. Taste, touch, smell, sight, hearing—all our senses play tricks on us. Why, then, do we place so much faith in them? And where can we turn to find the truth?

When the sages of Kabbalah tell us that the vast majority of what goes on in this universe lies beyond the realm of our senses and even beyond our understanding, they know well of what they speak. Of course, it might well be asked, "Why is it necessary or even prudent to consider that which we can never see?" The answer is that Kabbalah seeks to understand the source of all things. To the kabbalist, accepting the observable world as the totality of existence means cheating oneself out of the vast majority of life's possibilities.

The elements in daily events that often create so much chaos can be avoided when connection to the encircling Light exists within our consciousness. Once we begin to recognize the superconscious encircling Light as an essential aspect in the development of a fulfilled life, chaos can no longer instigate anger, frustration, or bewilderment. We suddenly gain a level of awareness in which we begin to experience wonder and awe in place of confusion and misery.

And in achieving this higher frame of awareness, we recognize the restricted vision of our five senses—because quantum perception lies beyond the grasp of our everyday finite consciousness. Activity originating in faraway places most certainly affects the activities of individuals, notwithstanding the distance that lies between them. Consequently, the future of any plan of action must remain uncertain and immersed in the likelihood that if anything can go wrong, it will.

Gaining connection with the superconscious encircling Light therefore requires all the tools and teachings of Kabbalah. Mastering our destiny involves, first and foremost, mastery of our universe and universal activity. Beyond the slightest doubt, conventional thinking on matters of this kind is severely inadequate to this task.

Common sense should tell us that the finite, physical manifestation of any event has little to do with the whole truth. Terms like "pull the wool over your eyes," "snow job," and "smokescreen" are commonly used to describe a covering over of the truth. To the kabbalist's way of thinking, our entire realm of existence in the material dimension is similarly covered over and concealed by curtains of negativity—called *klippot* in Hebrew—and hence is deemed illusory. *The Zohar* and the great kabbalist Rav Isaac Luria (known as the Ari) gave us a system with which to penetrate the curtains of illusion that surround this world, and with which we can find the infinite reality— the encircling Light—that lies within. Once we have understood these teachings of Kabbalah, we no longer need to accept at face value the lies that so commonly pose as truth. Rather than remain slaves to deception, we can become the masters of our fate.

JERUSALEM: WHAT IT WAS, WHAT IT IS, WHAT IT MEANS

For thousands of years, Jerusalem has been called the Holy City because the Holy Temple was located there. The kabbalistic comment on this is, "Why was the Holy Temple located in Jerusalem?" The physical expression of the Temple cannot determine underlying causes inasmuch as we are left with the question, "What brought about the Temple site in the first place?"

The Zohar clearly documents the link between the Temple and the City of Jerusalem. The initial reason for the Temple's location was related to the fact that the energy center of the universe abides in the Land of Israel. *The Zohar* tells us that the Temple and the Ark within the city of Jerusalem were receivers and conductors of cosmic energy-intelligence. When a circuit of energy flowed from this center, the universe and all of its infinite galaxies were in harmony. Chaos and violence did not exist.

The Temple of Jerusalem expressed something entirely different from the temples of other ancient peoples. What happened in Jerusalem affected everything on earth as well as throughout the cosmos. Jerusalem was and is the nucleus around which all the galaxies revolve. Jerusalem did not then, nor does it now, represent a religious ideology. Its physical structures merely symbolize a metaphysical thought energy-intelligence, just as the body represents the internal soul consciousness of humankind. In the final analysis, the body is a secondary manifestation. Our soul energy-intelligence is what motivates and animates body consciousness. And the sooner we come to this realization, the better our possibilities will be for reaching meaningful and lasting solutions to problems of every kind. Meanwhile, our present approach to problem solving has done little to fulfill the objectives necessary to ensure the well-being of the individual or of our society.

Superficial reasoning in determining cause and effect is a convenience of the five senses. This reasoning permits us to sit back comfortably, thinking we have worked things through. Little do we realize that, as Murphy's Law declares, "If anything can go wrong, it will go wrong." In keeping with this law, cracks in our reasoning are easily filled or replaced by the negative side.

Despite the often frustrating experience of trying to get to the "bottom of it all," every avenue must be pursued in efforts to determine primary causes. Complacency and shallow, ostrich-like feelings of denial provide only false solutions to our problems. The entire spectrum of quantum reality must be researched before we can come to any conclusions. The answer to the final "why" reveals the ultimate cause. This is our gateway not only to problem solving of every kind, but also to wisdom itself.

TIME TRAVEL

Only recently has science, using the authentic discoveries of modern physics as its foundation, seriously begun to address the possibility of time travel. In the past, time travel was the exclusive domain of science fiction. Now, however, even some highly regarded mainstream researchers are coming to recognize that time travel may well be possible, at least in theory. To be sure, the design of a time machine is not yet under consideration; scientists have enough problems trying to work out the kinks in time-travel theories. The key point, however, is that physicists have found nothing in the laws of physics that would prohibit time travel even as a concept.

So there currently exists the possibility that someday, someone might somehow do what science fiction characters now do only in books and movies: speed through hyperspace to a distant galactic outpost traveling faster than the speed of Light. Scientists tell us that if we could travel at the speed of Light, time would actually proceed into the past. An astronaut traveling at the speed of Light could even zoom into deep space and return before he left!

No one now disputes the basic science that Einstein revealed at the start of the 20th century: that time slows down for a moving object, as measured by an observer considered to be stationary. According to this theory, if one member of a pair of identical twins travels at Light speed to a distant star and back, he will return to find that his watch has been running slower during the journey and that his stay-at-home brother has aged more than he has.

This time-expansion effect has been confirmed by experiment. Atomic clocks taken on long jet rides have been found to lag five billionths of a second behind clocks that have remained on earth. It's clear that conventional laws of science are inadequate to the task of dealing with elastic time that can be extended or reduced, stretched or shrunk—not to mention realms in which time no longer exists, or in which subatomic particles actually travel back in time.

For the present, scientists think only in terms of the "time dilation"—that is, the slowing down of time such that, at the most, time becomes frozen. Time might come close to stopping, but scientists maintain that it can't be made to march backward, even in theory. An argument often made against the concept of two-way time travel has become known as the "grandfather paradox." A time traveler would encounter it if he returned to the past just in time to prevent the meeting of his own grandparents. This, in effect, would mean that he himself would never have been born. But if he had not been born, he could not have prevented the marriage of his grandparents or have been present to go back in time in the first place. If time travel is possible, how do we avoid violating causality? How can something go back to the past and affect its future in such a way as to prevent its backward journey through time?

Science fiction writers have dealt with this paradox by proposing that somehow we would be prevented from doing anything in the past that would affect our future in a way that couldn't be reconciled with time travel. Unfortunately, this proposal contradicts the very idea of time travel to the past. It asserts that you "can't have your cake and eat it too"—but in essence it is just another way of saying that we really haven't come up with any answers to the original problem.

While scientists and philosophers argue about the nature of time or question its reality, most of us continue to think of time as the duration of everyday processes. Einstein's theory of relativity, however, takes us beyond our daily experience, which is the basis of common sense and logic. Is it logical to recognize that if we were capable of traveling at the speed of Light, we would then return prior to our departure? If we could travel faster than Light, time would actually run backward. We would take a trip and return the day before we left. A theory that has such far-reaching implications, and that runs counter to our daily experiences, could never have entered the mainstream of scientific thought had it not been verified in many experiments. Relativity shattered once and for all the commonly accepted notion of absolute time. And in doing so, it opened the door to yet another reality—that of elastic time, which is completely dependent on the velocity of the observer.

Kabbalah goes one step further and declares that relativity is only the beginning of a true understanding of time. The state of our consciousness is yet another form of time travel. Words like "sooner," "later," and "now" are also expressions of time's relativity. What is "here and now" for one is "there and then" for another. From the perspective of a man who is late for an important appointment, time is rushing by at a breakneck pace, whereas from the standpoint of another man who is early for the same appointment, time may be dragging on interminably. How time is perceived depends on the perspective from which it is observed.

If the man who is late for his appointment were to be suddenly teleported to his destination, time would immediately be transformed from a restraining tyrant to a benign servant—one deserving of praise instead of complaints. Time would have brought all the parties together at the same instant, in the same place, for the same meeting. So while it is true that most of us cannot stem the tide of "time marches on," we can change our perception and understanding of that statement. And in so doing, we can significantly alter the course of our lives.

Imagine time as a river that runs from the far distant past into the far distant future. Imagine that the flow of the river is controlled by your wants and needs, your moods and emotions. When your thoughts are clear, so too are the waters of time. When you are agitated, the waters are agitated as well. When you are in a hurry (as was the man who was late for his appointment), the banks of the river are narrow and the waters are white-capped rapids. When you are at rest, the waters run cool and calm. When you are afraid, the waters are dark and ominous. When you are at peace, the waters are mirror-glass smooth.

THE ESSENCE OF TIME

What, then, is the essence of time? Is it a friend or an enemy? Is it our servant, a mere convenience by which we measure our lives, or a tyrant who rules over us with an iron fist? Do we use time, or does it use us? In truth, there is no single answer to this question. Time is what we make it through the power of our own perspective and awareness. And in this sense, time is no different from life itself.

Once we accept Einstein's revolutionary ideas of time, we encounter little difficulty accepting kabbalistic versions of time and time travel. If we could travel faster than Light, time would actually run backward. We could go on a trip and return the day before we left. We could also travel back to the days of our youth. In effect, we would have found the Fountain of Youth— our own unique and individual source of restoration and renewal. Myths surrounding the search for the Fountain of Youth have always proposed that it exists somewhere outside ourselves. However, if time ran in reverse—and physicists find no reason why it should not—dead people would come alive, trees would "ungrow," and shattered glass would put itself back together. If all this sounds quite amazing, try looking at it from a different perspective. Rather than ask how such things could possibly happen if time were to go forward, ask why they aren't happening right now. After all, physicists have yet to agree on a theory that explains why time goes forward at all. Theoretically, it could just as easily flow in the opposite direction.

From a kabbalistic standpoint—and from a scientific perspective as well—everything that has ever happened in the universe, everything that ever will happen, and everything that is happening right now has been unalterably determined from the first moment of time. The future may be uncertain in our minds, but it is already arranged in every minute detail. It is precisely this realization that brought about the differences that exist between Kabbalah and the yet-unverified precepts that science so blindly follows.

Scientists have declared that no human decision or action can change the destiny of a single atom. However free we may perceive ourselves to be, scientists tell us that everything we do is predetermined. All of existence is thus encapsulated, frozen into a single moment. Past and future have no real significance. Nothing actually changes.

The problem that science must acknowledge is this: If the arrow of time can point in either direction, then trying to unbreak an egg, grow younger, or make a river flow uphill should be a perfectly acceptable sequence of events. These events do not take place because the physical processes that occur in our world seem to be irreversible. You simply cannot make things "go backward." The kabbalistic worldview maintains, however, that human decisions can indeed change the fate of an atom—and much more.

The physical world, as we have discussed, conforms to the Heisenberg uncertainty principle. This universe exists as the "gathering place" for our illusions of certainty. It is here that time, space, and motion make their presence felt. Within this uncertain universe exists the fragmentation of time, where events seem to be irreversible and becoming younger simply does not happen.

From a kabbalistic perspective, however, the future does not exist as a separate entity. Growing younger indicates a creative process of reversibility, but the fallacy behind this idea lies in the fact that we have never aged to begin with. There is never a future period of aging, nor for that matter was there ever a past that saw us becoming older. There is nothing more to reality than the present!

THE SPEED OF LIGHT

With regard to time travel, the fundamental problem facing scientists today concerns inadequate propulsion with which to achieve or exceed travel at the speed of Light. Yet time travel, or traveling at the speed of Light, was not an uncommon experience for kabbalists in the past. *The Zohar* does not consider the problems associated with approaching the speed of Light to be an insurmountable obstacle. The solution lies not in producing propulsion that will approach the speed of Light, but rather in removing the barrier of that speed itself.

Amazingly enough, *The Zohar* presents a plan that would provide us with the capacity to travel the entire solar system as if it were our own backyard. Of course, this idea is no less incredible than the effect of transcontinental flight, which in the mid-20th century rapidly converted our once-formidable oceans and seas into little more than swimming holes!

The secret so clearly and simply stated in *The Zohar* is that the removal of the speed-of-Light barrier depends wholly on the removal of the "humanity barrier," represented by our hatred for and intolerance toward one another. The removal of physical barriers rests entirely on our ability to erase our spiritual limitations. Until the whole of humanity recognizes the necessity for removing these obstacles, however, those individuals who are already connected to the principle of "love your neighbor as yourself" should avail themselves now of the opportunity to connect to the Light revealed on Mount Sinai.

Let us therefore turn to the Zoharic revelations of time travel and to the time machine that is necessary for removing the speed-of-Light barrier. This process can be compared to the digging of a tunnel by a mechanism that disintegrates and vaporizes earth and stone, thereby permitting that tunnel to be completed in the little time it takes this spectacular mechanism to travel from one end of the tunnel to the other. The same principle applies to the Zoharic time machine. By "vaporizing" the speed-of-Light barrier, which is an expression of the Desire to Receive for Oneself Alone, all concepts of speed and distance disappear.

The process described above is very similar to what rockets undergo in outer space. The friction that is present in the earth's atmosphere is absent in space. Consequently, rockets can travel at speeds of up to 24,000 miles per hour. Of course, this is still not as fast as the speed of Light, because the speed-of-Light barrier exists in outer space as well.

With the Zoharic time machine, the essence of the speed-of-Light barrier—the Desire to Receive for Oneself Alone—is broken down and vaporized. The illusions of space and time are rendered nonexistent. Once this takes place, conventional distance and time cease to exist. We are instantly in two places at the same moment. We have succeeded in being as much in the past as we are in the present. As it is written in *The Zohar*:

> And when the Scroll is to be brought to the altar for reading on the Shabbat, it is incumbent upon all present to prepare themselves in awe, fear, trembling, and

in sweat. And to direct their hearts as if they were standing now on Mount Sinai to receive revelation and the Torah Scroll!

Just as the equations of the physical sciences express time as symmetrical (meaning that the equations work as well in one temporal direction as in the other), so too does *The Zohar* find no difficulty in stating the conditions required to move in reversed time. And as we have seen, reversed time means returning to the Revelation at Mount Sinai, where the Light first became manifest.

The prerequisites stipulated in *The Zohar* are quite similar to movies that portray individuals traveling back in a time machine, trembling, sweating, and fearful. Severe physical stresses cannot be avoided during flights into space and back to earth. Heavy vibrations and the forces of rapid acceleration start the journey off with intense strains. These are the very conditions mentioned in *The Zohar*.

WHAT LIES AHEAD?

The physics of the future lies beyond the dimensions of the physical reality of our world. This new physics will permit us to go beyond space and time in our analysis of the universe in which we find ourselves, to the point at which, it is hoped, "one day a door will open, no wider than the eye of a needle, and unto us shall open the supernal gates exposing the glittering interrelatedness of the universe with all its beauty and simplicity."

Although Kabbalah already clarifies many enigmatic aspects of nature, it remains simple. The kabbalistic vision of reality is based on an in-depth understanding of the Bible's coded narration and tales. Kabbalah's teachings reveal the underlying laws with which we can establish influence and control over our environment, and through which we can understand the power that nature has held over us.

Kabbalah thus teaches that our universe is perceived as fragmented only because humanity itself is fragmented. In the 1940s, science split off the atom for the first time—an event that was initially hailed as an immense breakthrough. Only now has it become evident that the use of nuclear power as an energy source is a grievous mistake. Nuclear energy, which requires the splitting of the atom, represents the most extreme and perilous example of technology reeling out of control. Let us therefore reexamine this once highly acclaimed solution to humanity's needs.

The first step taken toward splitting the atom lay in the thought of creating an energy far more powerful than anything that had ever before existed. When Einstein published his theory of relativity in 1905, he made this dream a possibility. But fragmented atoms can spell only darkness. The scientists involved in the development of man's most self-destructive system, from which there is no longer an escape, were in a state of robotic consciousness. They were merely reflecting humanity's destructive inclination and activities. They were being used to express the negative side. The disintegration of the atom began because of our ongoing inhumane actions toward our fellow man. The bombing of Hiroshima and Nagasaki was only the first consequence.

The long-term effects of nuclear power have yet to be felt.

For those of us who seek to enhance the welfare and well-being of humanity, kabbalistic techniques can prove to be a method by which we can avert the pitfalls that lie before us. These techniques can and will transform water that is undrinkable into water that will not cause us to suffer or undergo the negative effects of contamination. The points raised by the teachings of Kabbalah have been confirmed as going directly to the heart of any topic science is capable of reaching.

THE NEXT SCIENTIFIC REVOLUTION

Richard Feynman clearly stated that the probability that we will attain a true and deep understanding of the universe is highly unlikely. There is just too much "out there." So what hope does the future hold for us when everything we relate to or participate in is plagued with so much uncertainty?

The Newtonian mechanistic perception, which no longer dominates scientific thinking, was far too rigid. A complete revolution in the science of physics was therefore required to overturn it. But now, once again, radical change is necessary. Kabbalah and its doctrines are ready to replace uncertainty and illusion with the reality and wholeness of a true and eternally providential nature. Kabbalistic teachings provide the individual with the ability to create an internal, private inner universe—a totally new movie—in which all uncertainty, chaos, disorder, and destruction are revealed as ineffectual, illusory states.

The first step in this process lies in the realization that our own Ego is the force that threatens our very existence. Ego is the factor underlying the limited expression of our consciousness. Our ego convinces us that all our decisions and activities are the direct result of our own conscious mind and thought. Yet as corporate managers, we make decisions that are detrimental to the welfare of consumers. As business decision makers, we become nearsighted, unable to see beyond our egotistical positions and immediate rewards. As a result, nature as a whole suffers greatly for our inexcusable lack of desire to share on a quantum level.

The second step in the commitment process requires open-mindedness toward any and all information presented by kabbalistic teachings. At first, this might appear to be a simple matter. But considering the programming that most of us have undergone, our preconceived ideas are the most important factor standing in the way of our transformation. To overcome this obstacle, we will need monumental effort and commitment. The revision of our concepts and theories must be so radical that a question might arise as to whether our present system can endure it. Here again, however, let me repeat: From a kabbalistic viewpoint, our current perspective is outmoded. We must address ourselves again to fundamental truths and values. We must deal with human potentialities and integrate them into the underlying matrix of our entire global system.

CHAPTER TWO:
RESTRICTION

CREATION THROUGH RESTRICTION

The kabbalistic principle of mind over matter requires that we detach ourselves from the confines of physicality and connect ourselves to the positive energy-intelligence of celestial bodies. Humanity's finite aspect, which may be described as flesh and bones, is subject to Cartesian rules and regulations. However, our infinite being operates beyond physical jurisdiction. Whatever is finite is subject to pain, discomfort, and death. The infinite exists in an entirely different realm.

In order to connect with our infinite aspect—that is, with our own souls—we must pay homage to the original act of creation, which is Restriction. Through the channel of Restriction, it becomes possible for us to transcend space, time, and matter, including freedom from every form of pain and suffering. Physically, we are creatures of earth; spiritually we reside perpetually in the Endless. The finite part of us is subject to change, turmoil, pain, and suffering. Our higher aspect remains beyond the jurisdiction of physicality.

UNSEEN INFLUENCES

Kabbalah describes energy-intelligence as existing independently of time, space, and the laws of motion. It can best be understood as ongoing permutations of thought. The mind of a human being, therefore, is not only where information is stored; it is where energy-intelligence is created. Human consciousness acts upon energy-intelligent thought and transforms it into energy-intelligent matter.

What's more, the perceptions of each individual mind are programmed into the whole universal grid in such a way that those perceptions are instantly imposed on the minds of all humanity. If, for example, you're sitting at a table in a restaurant, the former occupants of that table will have instilled in it energy-intelligence that may be positive or negative—but in either case, you will surely be affected by it. When we rent or purchase a new home, we must recognize that the thought consciousness of the home's previous residents are permeating the space. Were they positive or negative people? I want to emphasize this point in order to highlight the many unseen influences that affect our lives and well-being. Although our attention is usually captured by our physical setting and by the conversation that currently occupies us, other energies have an impact on our thoughts and behavior, and they do so outside the realm of our conscious evaluation.

Fortunately, kabbalistic teachings allow us to become increasingly aware of the unseen influences that are very much a part of our human experience. These influences can penetrate whatever security shields have been placed in the universe for our protection, whether we call these shields immune systems or ozone layers. And certainly at this moment, we are vulnerable to the onslaught of negative energies.

As a way of life, Kabbalah offers unmatched tools and techniques for the restoration of our security shields and for creating balance within the cosmos. Applying these tools, however, takes effort. Living in accordance with Restriction and the Desire to Receive for the Purpose of Sharing is very demanding. As always, however, the principle of "no pain, no gain" applies. Lack of effort only creates a space for the Desire to Receive for Oneself Alone. Mere effort—stress—is not and cannot be a factor in the breakdown of our security shield. Vulnerability based on ignorance is much more damaging. It is crucial that we achieve an awareness of the unseen influences around us. We must understand how the mind can assist in promoting the welfare of the universe in general, and of humanity in particular.

THE CURE FOR ALL ILLS

The Zohar assures us that we really can reduce the universe's apparent complexity into a single thought-intelligence. To begin to understand this, however, we must first grasp the fact that the two fundamental and seemingly opposing forces that manifest in innumerable ways—including the seeming attraction and repulsion of a magnet's poles—are not really distinct from one another. Instead, they are different manifestations of the same underlying interaction that exists in the realm of the encircling Light.

This cosmic glue—the single unifying energy-intelligence that governs all interactions in the cosmos—is known in Hebrew by the code name *Masakh D'Khirik*, or the Central Column. Its energy is that of Restriction, the amazing cure for all ills in both the celestial and terrestrial realms.

Can it really be that simple? Yes, it can, and it is. The idea that we can reduce the staggering complexity of the universe to its essential simplicity through the power of our thought-intelligence is, to say the least, an exciting possibility. The words of *The Zohar*, "as above, so below," go a long way toward describing a universe in which all manifestations, both physical and metaphysical, are tied together in a web of interconnected relationships, each apart from and yet part of the all-embracing unity.

CREATING THE MOVIE YOU WANT TO SEE

For the most part, despite the huge advances that have taken place in medicine and other forms of scientific endeavor, we have not yet found any viable means of protecting our physical and mental well-being against all forms of assault. It would seem that there are just too many factors involved to allow for such definitive protection. So we act and pray—mostly pray—that our hopes will prevail over our fears.

But who can say for sure that the results we seek are those that are really best suited to our needs? With this thought in mind, we can see how much time and effort are consumed by seeking to know the unknowable!

Our despair and frustration are incalculable. Connection with the superconscious encircling Light adds a new dimension—namely, that of precise determinism. But everything depends on whether we apply the restriction-sharing energy-intelligence of human activity or, instead, choose to indulge in the Desire to Receive for Oneself Alone. Selfish activity creates an environment of uncertainty in which even seemingly flawless plans become subject to the whims of the quantum universe.

When we act with the energy-intelligence of Restriction, how-ever, we can access the superconscious encircling Light as the movie for our daily existence. When this occurs in conjunction with the use of kabbalistic tools and teachings, everything becomes significantly improved, even beyond our most opti-mistic plans. The superconscious removes all the rough edges and replaces any doubts or uncertainties that might beset us.

The Zohar drives home the point that if our negative human activity prevails, a severance takes place between the continuity phase of reality and our human plans and hopes. Kabbalistic techniques, plus the positive energy-intelligence of Restriction, are our links to certainty—that is, to the realm of the encircling Light. Both for ourselves and for the world, the implications and benefits of this quantum superconscious are literally with-out limits.

CHAPTER THREE:

REINCARNATION

"HAVEN'T WE SEEN THIS BEFORE?"

In everything we do, we manifest aspects of ourselves from former lifetimes. Life for most of us represents a remake of a movie in which we previously acted, a reprise of tasks attempted earlier in which we somehow failed.

In the 21st century, humanity is merely living a motion picture rerun over and over again. Although human behavior is genetically determined to a significant degree, the *Tikkune* directs and dictates our everyday thought patterns, feelings, and activities. Our behavior, decisions, and reactions to our environments, as well as our most profound fears and moments of enjoyment, evolve directly from the results of accumulated lifetimes.

The law of *Tikkune* is really the law of fair play. By being permitted to sojourn in the physical world, the soul is given an opportunity to correct misdeeds performed in a previous lifetime. Unfortunately, it usually takes us far too many lifetimes to complete a *Tikkune*. Our lessons are patiently repeated day after day, year after year, and even lifetime after lifetime until the knowledge we have ignored comes crashing down on us, sometimes in a devastating fashion. And even then, many of us do not fully grasp the implications of the experience or make the necessary correction. History reveals that humanity knows and has learned almost nothing. For example, we still lift our hands against our fellow human being without realizing that warfare does not spare the victor.

I am aware that these ideas challenge the conventional view of social scientists, who contend that it is culture and upbringing that shape human nature. Kabbalah teaches that every instant of our lives is fully determined by the cosmic forces prevailing at that time. Our actions are indeed controlled by the cosmos, but only to the extent that they were manifested in a prior lifetime. For example, if an individual committed crimes against humanity in a previous incarnation, his soul will return and will be faced with the same type of challenge he failed to meet in his past lifetime. He will now be given a new opportunity: either to exercise free will and thwart the cosmic scenario that determined and manifested his present life movie, or to fall before it once again.

These negative frames of reference, established in a former lifetime, are manifested by cosmic activities at the time of a person's birth. Essentially, the cosmos merely presents the movie of our past lifetime in the form of a framework and an opportunity. The cosmos itself is not the cause of our life movie's structure; this has already been determined by our former lifetime. The set of circumstances occurring in our present lifetime is a result of the accumulation of cosmic influences coming together now, and affecting our *Tikkune* requirements.

THAT WAS THEN; THIS IS NOW

Here we might ask the question, "What are the chances of succeeding this time around when we have already failed in countless prior lifetimes?" These negative frames of reference that we ourselves created provide us with an opportunity to exercise free will and achieve our true purpose in the world. If these negative cosmic forces did not exist, man would simply conform to a programmed version of existence, leaving no room for the passions, animosities, or other characteristics that distinguish us from robots. Yet while cosmic negativity does arouse evil behavior, this powerful influence can and should be regulated and controlled. This is the obligation of free-thinking and free-choosing individuals. But as history has demonstrated, man has failed to master his destiny. Now, however, because the teachings of the Kabbalah are being made available to all, man can overcome this failure.

A further question of interest is, "Why now?" Our environment at present is highly unstable—and with recent scientific advances, we have become acutely aware of internal metaphysical activity that seems to engender even more uncertainty. Here again, by virtue of these scientific advances, we are becoming much more enlightened. We now demand to know the cause of the apparent instability and uncertainty in our lives. And this is where Kabbalah can literally bring about the transformation of humankind. Although Kabbalah has for centuries been a carefully guarded secret, the time has now come for it to reach the world as a whole with its simple yet powerful message. In the final analysis, only that which is understood by everyone can be considered true knowledge.

THE ASTROLOGICAL PERSPECTIVE

Kabbalah's view of astrology is dramatically different from anything you may have heard or read on this topic. Conventional astrology contends that an individual takes a course of action because of the arrangement of the stars. By contrast, Kabbalah teaches that the *Tikkune* process of karmic correction places us in an astrological position so that the stars will point us in the necessary direction. Birth charts—or "horoscopes"—are a pictorial expression of a metaphysical interface.

The various scenes of our past lifetimes always continue to exist as metaphysical channels of energy. When, in the present, we act in a negative manner that corresponds to negative behavior in a past life, we become infused with negative energy-intelligence. But this is not just malice on the part of the universe. Our prior negative activity is superimposed on our present life experiences in order to provide us with an opportunity to make a correction, or a *Tikkune*. Moreover, each day of our current lifetime corresponds to a particular moment in a former incarnation. If, for example, today is your 26th birthday, the astral bodies will transmit the movie of your behavior on precisely this day in a prior incarnation.

Despite the inviolability of the basic pattern of our destiny, we also have a degree of freedom that is almost without limitation. We can determine how the *Tikkune* process will take place within our present lifetime. The birth chart reveals the obstacles and restrictions that will prevent us from feeling free. In addition, shortsightedness, bigotry, and other negative attitudes may prevent us from making use of the tools that are available for karmic change and spiritual growth. These barriers are of our own making. But because we created them, we can also shatter them and ascend to higher levels of consciousness.

Let's return for a moment to the phenomenon of cosmic bombardment that so often robs us of inner peace. What is the source of the complex and turbulent thoughts that appear in the subconscious mind? The subconscious does not reason. To the contrary, it merely responds to input from a prior lifetime or from many prior lifetimes. Our mental static now is an accumulation of what was going on then. If we compare this subconscious process to the workings of a film projector, we discover that the machine does the "thinking" for us. Most people never realize this. The tools and teachings of Kabbalah, however, give us the ability first to become aware of cosmic attack, and then to make changes that will eventually bring that attack to a halt.

The Zohar states, "Each unit of consciousness or intelligence returns to its former unmanifest position after having served its purpose." Thus, both our mundane universe and our own physical bodies reflect a constant back-and-forth movement between earthbound reality and the cosmic realm. By contrast, the cosmic realm constitutes the timeless, spaceless realm we inhabit if we are to be true masters of our own destiny.

This again demonstrates the great Zoharic truth, "As above, so below." As in the metaphysical universe, so in the physical world. The barrage of thought energy to which we are subjected originates in this lifetime from the cosmos. However, Kabbalah reveals that the cosmos is the primary source for good and evil, for health and disease, for serenity and chaos. As long as we focus our attention on the symptoms, we will fail to discover the underlying cause. Yet we have been programmed by our culture to believe that anything more than temporary relief is probably impossible. And as long as we continue to believe this, real change is impossible.

FROM VULNERABILITY TO IMMUNITY

Misfortune, in whatever manifestation it appears, is the direct result of our negative attitudes in present or former lifetimes. That we can change the direction of our misfortune is what the study of Kabbalah is all about. However, the kabbalist knows quite well the time spans during which the negative side has been given dominion in our universe, and it thus provides the security shield that can and will protect us from this devastating onslaught. Embracing negative attitudes essentially involves connecting with and embracing the negative side as a whole. The creation of an affinity with this dark environment prevents any progress from being made in the removal of misfortune, whether it takes the form of ill health, family problems, financial instability, or other calamities.

This brings us to a renewed understanding of vulnerability, a concept we explored earlier. There are two conditions that must be met to guarantee mastery of our lives and destinies. first, our attitude toward our fellow man must be one of humility. Thus, Jacob understood that in order for him to overcome the essence of the negative side, he must "humble himself before Esau."

Second, we must don a security shield when negative energy-intelligences prevail within the cosmos, however strongly we may boast of our wholesome, positive attitudes. Here let us refer once again to Jacob, who had a serious encounter with the negative side. Although Jacob was decidedly the victor in this encounter, he nonetheless suffered a severe injury. He had exposed himself, albeit deliberately, to danger. And the absence of a security shield demonstrated the vulnerability of even so powerful an individual as Jacob.

Here *The Zohar* reveals an understanding of the enigmatic question of why one person is vulnerable and another is not. Consider, for example, the cosmic effects and influences on the development of cancer. When scientific researchers propose a theory that "happy people do not have cancer," they are by no means incorrect. However, as is often the case in the biomedical paradigm, the physical, manifested condition is taken as the cause rather than the effect..

Granted that happy people avoid the scourge of cancer, the question that we must ask ourselves is, "Why are some people happy and others not?" In essence, we must explore and search out the essential cause. Only when the whys and wherefores of answers are resolved may we assume that we have come upon a primary cause.

There are essentially two basic factors that contribute to humanity's vulnerability, and both are channeled through the cosmos. Before we investigate the agents responsible for our becoming vulnerable, however, let me make it clear once again that humanity is potentially in a position to convert vulnerability into immunity.

The problem of vulnerability is not, from a kabbalistic perspective, a question of who will fall into the category of being lucky or unlucky. Rather, we were exposed to the misfortunes of vulnerability when in past lifetimes we failed to overcome the Desire to Receive for Oneself Alone!

Exposure to the traumas and misfortunes that accompany vulnerability takes place in this lifetime within precisely the same time frames we experienced them in prior incarnations. If, in a previous lifetime, we failed in our *Tikkune* process to restrict the urge to steal, we will experience in this lifetime another free-choice opportunity to determine whether or not we will overcome the urge to steal and succeed by Restriction. If we fail, we will have created fragmentation, limitation, "empty space," and concealment of the Creator. This gap represents vulnerability—an opening through which the negative side makes its entry.

From a spiritual perspective, vulnerability is an area of our being in which the future has been overshadowed by the past. Vulnerable people are placed in danger by a genetic "time bomb" that has been passed from a former lifetime to the present. When modern medicine determines that an individual is at risk for an illness because of a single missing or defective gene, measures can sometimes be taken to prevent the actual onset of the disease. Yet more basic questions are rarely asked, either by the physician or by the patient. Why, for example, was the individual put into this position in the first place? Why was he or she born into a family with this genetic disposition? What does my situation have to do with the purpose for which I am in the world? We should not allow our questions to be limited by biomechanical models. Any lethal legacy must be traced beyond the materialist blueprint for life.

In the physical realm, there are many reasons a group of people might be bonded together, including racial, geographic, or family ties. Kabbalah teaches us, however, that these relationships are not the primary causes of any negativity that may be present within a group. It teaches, instead, that these people have been bound together because of *Tikkune* issues from prior lifetimes. A physical ailment may point to the cause of the difficulty, but it cannot be considered to be a primary cause in itself.

With this in mind, we can now understand that flaws in DNA— or misfortunes of any kind—are a direct result of failure in the *Tikkune* process. For every action there is a similar and opposite reaction, and this is every bit as true on the spiritual level as it is in classical Newtonian physics. Pain caused to others results in pain for the perpetrator. As always, however, a present difficulty also represents a potential opportunity. When misfortune from a prior lifetime projects itself into the movie of our current lifetime, the unrolling film can be altered by a demonstration of **Restriction**.

Restriction therefore plays a major role in the body's resistance to disease. Producing natural antibodies—the soldier cells that defend against illness—is the task assigned to the consciousness of Restriction.

Although the *Tikkune* process predisposes us to vulnerability, Restriction allows us to overcome the predetermined script. Restriction is the basis for a new movie in which a tragic ending can be transformed into something of a very different and highly positive nature.

The time, place, and circumstances for incarnated vulnerability are determined by an orchestration of the cosmos. Therefore, a well-made and meticulously read natal chart can be an invaluable tool for spiritual growth. A skilled astrologer can pinpoint specific openings and opportunities for the "reshooting" of our *Tikkune* movie. Yet even in the absence of such tools, we must treat misfortune, whenever it comes our way, as an opportunity for Restriction. For in so doing, we can stave off the potential effects of any illness or misfortune. An ounce of prevention is indeed worth a pound of cure!

The kabbalistic principle of "no coercion in spirituality" tells us that the Light cannot enter the vessel of our being unless we have prepared ourselves through the *Tikkune* process. No one can be forced to connect with the Light of the Creator, because this connection can take place only as an act of free will. The same principle permits us free will to exercise the power of Restriction against the Desire to Receive for Oneself Alone.

RETURNING SOULS

To understand what is really taking place, we must engage the kabbalistic teachings that concern returning souls. No mystery in the universe is as astonishing as the infinite returning and repeated behavior of its inhabitants.

Fundamental evolutionary precepts have scarcely changed throughout the course of history. We have witnessed civilizations rise and fall, yet basic life forms have endured essentially unchanged for vast periods of time. Even in our rapidly changing society, we, as well as all other life forms, continue to seek out the same things prior generations sought. Conservatism and stability remain the rule for most of the world's species. This is true both mentally and physically. Is our frame of mind really different from that of our counterparts from the Middle Ages? Have human psychological needs really changed through the centuries? Do we really better ourselves through "progress," which becomes more complex with each passing year? In most respects, the answer is no.

Consequently, it is extremely exciting to discover information that can bridge the gap between the phenomenon of material progress and the absence of change in terms of personal fulfillment. For this information, we again turn to *The Zohar*: "Rav Shimon Bar Yohai said, 'Companions, the time has arrived to reveal diverse hidden and secret mysteries in regard to the transmigration of souls.'" The Ari also emphasized this kabbalistic doctrine when he stated the following: "No individual can ever achieve a completed phase of repentance and correction until he becomes knowledgeable of the unconscious root psychological processes of the soul along with the knowledge of former lifetimes."

NOT A SEQUEL, BUT A NEW PRODUCTION

Let us now explore some of humanity's incarnations as described by the Ari, Rav Isaac Luria. Following the sin of Adam, Rav Luria explains, Adam's multiple souls were incarnated in the generation of the Deluge. Consequently, these same individuals enacted the identical movie of their prior incarnation. They, likewise, did not complete their *Tikkune*. This is indicated by the verse, "And the Lord repented that He created Adam (Man) on the earth, and it grieved him at his heart." The souls of Adam were then incarnated into the generation of the Tower of Babel. This is expressed in scriptures through the verse, "And the Lord came down to see the city and the tower which the children of Adam built." If we could only learn to cooperate with the movement of the universe and with the steadfast expansion of evolution, our spiritual growth would blossom. Only then could we achieve the paradise that the Tower of Babel so brazenly attempted to reach.

It is also unfortunate that so few of us wish to take advantage of the memory of experiences we have already had. We hesitate to delve into our own natures for fear of what we may find there. With the study of Kabbalah, these fears gradually dissipate to a point at which we can begin to take control over our present actions, our past mistakes, and our future destinies. Most important, we can gain power over the hostile environment that we consider home. Rather than experience constant confusion in our stream of consciousness, we can restructure our movie so that events in the inner world begin to come forth in a much more coherent way.

THE ATOM AS AN IDEA

To understand human nature, we must first study not only its physical and psychological dimensions but also its metaphysical aspects. To accomplish this, however, we will need enormous concentration if we are to sift through the maze of unnecessary and sometimes misleading information. Today we are so thoroughly inundated with irrelevant data that the task of separating the important from the unimportant often becomes overwhelming. The Age of Aquarius has introduced new phenomena that were unthinkable only a century ago. The atom as an idea —as an invisible entity beneath the realm of physical manifestation—is already mentioned in the Talmud. And in the 18th century, Newton wrote that "the Lord at the outset created matter in solid, hard, impenetrable, moving particles, of such sizes and figures, and with other properties, and in such proportion to space, as most conducive to the end to which He formed them."

James Clerk Maxwell, the Scottish physicist, was equally dedicated to the Newtonian idea of a "hard, impregnable" mechanical atom. In 1873, he wrote, "Though in the course of ages catastrophes have occurred and may yet occur in the heavens, though ancient systems may be dissolved and new systems evolved out of their ruins, the atoms out of which the sun and other celestial bodies are built remain unbroken and unworn."

By the end of the 19th century, the German physicist Max Planck was certain that if atoms existed, they could not be purely material entities. Planck believed that the essence universe lay beyond physicality. Furthermore, Planck and those who followed him viewed our universe as in a state of entropy, slowly moving toward chaos and ultimate dissolution. Quantum physics changed all this but at the same time left physicists with a black box filled with more unanswered questions than ever before. The prior vision of a universe moving toward death and decay was replaced by a new perspective in which the universe could run equally well backward or forward. Theoretically, a butterfly could turn back into a caterpillar and an old man into a child.

Unfortunately, this viewpoint provides no explanation for the fact that such things do not actually appear to happen. To date, for example, no old man has ever been observed to revert back to being a child. However, the doctrine of reincarnation states that the old man does in fact turn into a child in the sense that he is ultimately reborn as a "new" human being. The illusory period spanning death to rebirth belongs in a new frame of reference with which humanity must become acquainted. This "middle period" might be compared to the time a passenger on a subway train spends getting on at one station and traveling through darkness to arrive at the next. Simply because the train is unnoticed between stations does not in any way alter its trajectory to its destination, much less the train's actual existence.

The same principle holds for soul traveling along the *Tikkune* route of destiny. At death, the soul, like the train, seems to disappear for a short time between stops. The physical body disappears as well, but it is only the physical body that passes out of existence. Science, however, has yet to achieve awareness of this reality, just as it has lagged behind in other areas. Thus, science has essentially no moral guidelines. What oath of ethics do scientists impose upon themselves? Their work can be far more devastating than that of the medical profession. The Hippocratic oath brings some sense of responsibility to physicians, but other disciplines operate without any constraints whatsoever.

GENES, GENETICS, AND *TIKKUNE*

We have seen that the final form of any human structure is determined by the *Tikkune* process, which is an expression of an individual's actions in prior lifetimes. It is now necessary to consider the extent to which parents affect the development of their offspring. With modern techniques, it has become possible to demonstrate that genes direct the development and function of every part of the human body. All human behavior results from a complex interplay of environment and heredity—and data from studies done in the early 1950s points to the crucial role of heredity in physical and psychological development.

Can this finding be seen as contradictory to kabbalistic teachings? Kabbalah tells us that the *Tikkune* process—and not genetics—is the principal factor underlying intelligence, personality, and resistance or susceptibility to various diseases.

The *Tikkune* doctrine, however, stipulates only that the soul requires a proper setting for the execution of the correction process. From a kabbalistic perspective, the individual characteristics of any person derives essentially from the thoughts of his or her parents at the time of conception.

We must then question why it is that characteristics such as height, skin pigmentation, and intelligence seem to be so thoroughly a product of hereditary factors. If, as was mentioned, the mental computer that arranges the complete printout of the human being bases its input on one's particular range of prior incarnations, why do genetic studies indicate that heredity plays a such a key role in determining the above characteristics?

To answer this, it must first be understood that there are many different genes, and while each of them may exert only a small effect on an individual, all are nevertheless operative. It is therefore difficult to conclusively ascertain the impact of heredity. In addition, these characteristics do respond readily to variations in the environment that may conceal or alter the genetic effects. Consequently, a person exposed to the geography of the equator for a length of time may appear darker than his or her genes might actually indicate. Or an individual genetically predisposed to obesity may, if starved, be considerably thinner than a well-nourished person genetically inclined to slimness.

The concept of *Tikkune*, as seen through the eyes of the kabbalist, does not conflict with the idea of genetic transmission, if in fact such transmission is genetically necessary. What appears as genetic similarity may actually be the result of a soul returning after death to find the particular environment that is conducive to achieving the *Tikkune* process.

A hereditary disease such as hemophilia, which is the result of a defective gene transferred from a parent, does not conflict with a person's correction process. If the *Tikkune* requires this condition and environment, then the returning soul must locate them—and they will be similar to those it left behind in a former incarnation.

THE PROBLEM OF BIRTH TRAUMA

Consider the following shocking events. A 15-year-old Maryland boy walked into his parents' garage and hanged himself. The entire community was stunned. A 13-year-old boy in Mexico City set himself afire, and a confused neighborhood asked why. These were young people who had never seemed to be in any particular psychic pain. They had seemingly been coping well with the usual pains of adolescence. To friends and family, their deaths were inexplicable and tragically premature. And to psychiatrists and psychologists studying the phenomenon, they were another statistic in the growing epidemic of teenage suicides.

There is a body of research indicating that the tendency toward suicide, as well as vulnerability to drug addiction, may be linked to traumatic birth experiences. When considering the growing suicide rate in the United States, which has increased most dramatically among young people, we must make every effort to determine why this is taking place. According to the National

Center for Health Statistics, one American teenager attempts suicide every 78 seconds. Although these statistics are chilling, the idea of attributing this epidemic to the stress of modern life fails to satisfy many researchers. After all, stress in our society affects all, not just some. Obviously statistics do not tell us why some young people are taking their lives while others are not— even when environmental factors are the same.

It is therefore encouraging to learn that some researchers believe traumas suffered at birth may be imprinted within the unconscious. These traumas might be responsible, they say, for a compulsive urge to repeat the trauma during adolescence. In the 1920s, psychoanalyst Otto Rank proposed a similar theory to connect birth experience with neuroses. This idea was quickly denounced by Rank's peers, who commented that his ideas about birth trauma made about as much sense as astrology.

As a matter of fact, from a Zoharic perspective, birth traumas do relate to astrology. In fact, birth traumas are the direct result of astrological influences. Here we are again reminded of the kabbalistic principle that physical manifestations should never be used to determine primary causes.

Ignorant of this principle, sociologists researching problems such as the increase in suicide implicate everything from heavy-metal music to violent films. Yet all the while they fail to take notice of the metaphysical, prephysical realm of thought. After all, do we indulge in any physical activity without prior thought, however fleeting it might be? This is a critical concept: that the metaphysical precedes the physical, and that the metaphysical is constantly moving the whole of the cosmos. Yet researchers continue to fall into the trap of claiming that physicality is a primary cause of behavior.

An intensive research program conducted by Dr. Bertil Jacobson at Stockholm's Karolinska Institute produced data indicating that events surrounding an individual's birth may influence a subsequent decision to commit suicide. Dr. Jacobson's results were even more specific than he had anticipated. In one study, he found that suicide was more closely associated with birth trauma than with any of the other 11 risk factors for which he had tested, such as socioeconomic status, parental alcoholism, and broken homes. Dr. Jacobson also found a correlation between the type of birth trauma an individual had suffered and the mode of suicide. For example, he found that those who had asphyxiated themselves, whether by hanging, gas poisoning, or strangulation, were four times as likely to have suffered oxygen deficiency at birth. In a similar manner, 20% of those who had chosen to end their lives by mechanical means, such as with guns or knives, had experienced birth trauma such as breech presentation or forceps delivery at birth. Dr. Jacobson also discovered that future addicts were born in hospitals in which doctors chose to administer barbiturates and other drugs to women in labor.

How can physical trauma at birth, or brief periods of exposure to a drug, produce self-destructive behavior in adolescence? Most of us cannot remember anything that took place in the early years of life, let alone traumatic births. As a possible answer to this, some have suggested that traumatic experiences suffered at birth may somehow be imprinted in the brain. It is further hypothesized that this imprinting is responsible for a compulsive urge to repeat the trauma during adolescence.

But the real problem, as seen through the eyes of the kabbalist, is this: "What caused the mother to have the particular traumatic birth in the first place?" Or "Why do some expectant mothers choose drug-free childbirth and others do not?"

At birth, the brain of a human infant is not yet fully developed. Yet the mental and physical achievements seen during infancy are almost miraculous in their scope. Babies learn to turn over, sit up, crawl, and walk. Random babbling turns into words. From baby steps to gymnastics, in the first few years of life we witness miracles that have thus far eluded scientific understanding.

When science fails us, let us turn to *The Zohar*:

> There is the commandment to assign the death sentence, which is four in nature: by the sword, by strangulation, by stoning, and by burning. To whom does the Bible address itself? To Samael, the Dark Lord!

Here, in just a few words, *The Zohar* provides us with penetrating insight into the devastating traumas of uncommon deaths. These four causes of unnatural death have one thing in common: If an individual has succumbed to the energy-intelligence of the negative side by not restricting a particular Desire to Receive for Oneself Alone—and if this particular failure warrants the consequence of one of these four modes of death—

then, when the soul returns in the next incarnation, a traumatic birth will point to the kind of death the person underwent in a previous lifetime.

This is a truly startling revelation, and it illuminates an area that science has kept in darkness. Once again, we see the awesome power of insight provided for humanity by the Bible, when deciphered by the Kabbalah. Everything has an essential, underlying cause. There is a reason both for why things happen and for how they happen. But neither our five senses nor the views of conventional science can disclose these reasons, despite the fact that they affect our existence every day in the physical world.

CHAPTER FOUR:

MIND

THE MYSTERY WITHIN US

How should we view the mystery of the mind? Most researchers conclude that the mind and its functions, including thought and consciousness, are nothing more than integrated expressions of the brain's physical activities. But these mechanistic conclusions are no more than speculation, for there is in fact no evidence that "mind" is the mere functioning of the brain cells and nerves. What defies explanation is how information sensed by our nerve receptors—whatever that means—converges within the substance of our brains to become the subject and substance of thought. Unable to account for this, researchers choose to treat the phenomenon of mind as untouchable, lying beyond the reach of scientific investigation. They cannot explain how the mind functions, much less how we can use it more efficiently. In truth, mind functions are not determined by the precise mechanics of the brain's myriad nerve connections. Consequently, deterministic science can never account for every activity and phenomenon of consciousness.

Despite many years of research into the workings of memory, for example, the brain's ability to store information and to recall it on demand remains shrouded in mystery. The manner in which the brain keeps data in an orderly sequence is startling in its complexity. The memory stores of the brain are filled with information from every experience in life.

Equally remarkable is the power of the mind to retrieve pertinent information about these experiences from its endless memory bank. Like the most sophisticated computer imaginable, the mind identifies some quality of a concept and then directs a search for the appropriate word or phrase. The concept then appears, whole and coherent, in the conscious mind. Other phenomena of the brain-mind, such as intuition, love, and loyalty, are also startlingly complex. And then there are the unusual states of mind, such as dreams, illusions, and sensations of peace, joy, and fulfillment. Who pushes the button that triggers these mental experiences at particular moments of our lives, and why?

The kabbalistic perspective on mind-brain functions challenges conventional notions of the origin and essence of the mind. To be sure, Kabbalah's ideas may initially seem strange and even foreign. Yet if I am to make a serious and much-needed contribution to this critical area of inquiry, these ideas must be presented. I will therefore attempt to do so as clearly and concisely as possible. In sum, a human being may be seen as an information-processing organism whose various traits are closely tied to the complexity of the data presented from an environment of former lifetimes.

The mind-brain system is a complex system of interconnected, interdependent structures and functions projecting an already-produced film. The mind-brain can process any information at all, at once, faster and more reliably than can any computer. But the initial stages of processing always take place outside our awareness, as part of a program that has already been finalized long before any conscious processing ever occurs. It is for these reasons that kabbalists have always recognized the dominion of robotic consciousness over egocentric awareness. This conscious awareness, which plays no role in the initial and final stages of any process, has enslaved us for too long by convincing us that we are indeed in control of our fates, destinies, and decisions. The kabbalistic view—that reincarnation and the *Tikkune* process determine our behavior—has yet to gain general acceptance. But that day will arrive.

THE HIDDEN UNIVERSE OF MIND

The idea that virtually every human being uses only five percent of his or her brain power has long been accepted by the scientific community. Yet scientific researchers do not even attempt to investigate consciousness, the most dramatic of all mental functions. To the contrary, consciousness, if it is considered at all, is seen as a later and sometimes optional stage of cognitive information processing.

In the Zoharic view of this complex matter, the mind comprises a hidden "universe" of activities. Both science and Kabbalah agree that the mind performs complex pattern-recognition tasks and conducts operations that control our awareness of the environment. The mind also determines which intentions we wish to pursue and which actions we undertake. But Kabbalah teaches that the mind even directs experiences that seem to originate from beyond our reach, such as whether we live in wealth or in poverty. It is, in fact, perfectly logical that these experiences should be ascribed to the mind. If a man suffers poverty, for example, is it not because he failed to recognize some element that would have ensured the success of his business? Yet this is an "unconscious" process in the deepest sense of the word. In truth, the mind is arranged by unseen forces that are constantly structuring and restructuring reality. We, of course, are unaware that this process is even taking place. We perceive only the finished version of reality, which we conclude has always been that way.

MIND INTO MATTER

On the surface of everyday life, things often seem to be devoid of arrangement or form. Upon closer examination, however, there would appear to be a hidden order. Consider Morse-code messages. To anyone unfamiliar with it, Morse code would appear to be no more than a random jumble of sounds. To its practitioners, however, the code represents an intelligent signal. When information is encoded, it can be extremely difficult to decipher.

In the same manner, two parallel universes have been identified: the "Tree of Life" reality—the true, ordered level of consciousness—and the "Tree of Knowledge of Good and Evil," which is the illusory reality in which randomness, uncertainty, chaos, rot, disorder, illness, and misfortune make their presence felt. Which will we choose? And make no mistake—the choice is indeed ours.

An important theory of modern physics tells us that a physical object does not exist until observation brings it into being. In other words, only when I see a chair or a tree do those objects become real, and not before. The chair exists and doesn't exist, depending on whether it's observed.

Of course, this principle of two realities was presented long ago in *The Zohar*. Not only "mind over matter" but also "mind creates matter" have always been foundations of kabbalistic teachings.

In the biblical Book of Exodus, the principle of mind over matter is clearly illustrated by the ability of both Aaron and the Egyptian magicians to turn their rods into snakes. And lest we think that this episode was merely a parlor trick or an instance of the hand being quicker than the eye, *The Zohar* emphatically states that this was indeed a case of something turning into something else as a result of the power of the mind. Thus, in *The Zohar's* interpretation of the biblical verse, the rods actually did become serpents. We have all heard about the illusions of Harry Houdini, but illusions of this kind were not taking place in Egypt. Rather, awesome power was being exerted over the molecular and atomic structure of matter.

THE POWER OF THE INNER WORLD

You have a soul, and you should learn how to use it. There are really two levels of human existence: the internal soul consciousness, which is the true reality, and the external consciousness of the body and physicality in general, which is no more than a highly convincing illusion.

Prior to the sin of Adam, the entire universe was connected to the Creator, unlimited by space and time and unfettered by entropy and death. Body consciousness was completely dominated by soul consciousness. With the fall of Adam, however, body consciousness asserted itself, dragging down not only Adam but the entire the world as well. As his descendants, we have been struggling to regain the Eden of creation ever since.

There are many states of consciousness, and not all of them are benign. But because we can never completely separate ourselves from the universe, even the lowest of these states contains immense power that we must not take lightly. As it travels through the myriad levels that make up the metaphysical universe, the soul's only means of dealing with this power is to gain Oneness with the Creator. And the best and only road maps for reaching that goal are the teachings of Kabbalah and the revelations of *The Zohar*. *The Zohar*, with its careful scrutiny of the physical and spiritual anatomy of the individual, allows us to learn exactly what exists both within our consciousness and at the farthest reaches of the galaxies.

In particular, two remarkable revelations emerge in *The Zohar*. The first is the concept that we ourselves are the producers and directors of the great movie of the universe. The second is that all of humanity—both collectively and individually—are microcosms of everything in both the celestial and earthly realms of the universe.

Mechanistic thinkers may shake their heads in wonder at these precepts, but *The Zohar* is very clear in this regard: Humanity is inseparable from the universe as a whole, and the cosmos itself consists of soul and body consciousness.

This is a truly startling revelation. Attaching the idea of con-

sciousness to the cosmos is the most daring of all Zoharic dec-
larations. Exemplifying this idea, Rav Shimon Bar Yohai
achieved an extremely high degree of consciousness. He found
no difficulty in defining precisely what was taking place at any
level of reality. Without regard to space or time, he could access
information that clearly revealed both the future and the past.
Now that we ourselves are moving into the Aquarian Age, how
can we go about gathering this kind of information?

The Zohar, of course, gives us the answer to this question in its
description of the intimate relationship between the celestial
realm of the cosmos and the terrestrial realm of man. This
description also explains our fascination with the "unknowns"
of galactic space—a fascination that has existed for as long as we
have taken note of the structure and order of the universe. This
preoccupation arose when a fundamental awareness of the
dimension of the celestial realm and its profound influence on
our affairs became firmly established.

Although many attempts have been made in the past 300 years
to explain the intricately designed universe we now inhabit,
these attempts have left many conclusions hanging on a thread.
Scientists continue to cling to the belief that the key to understanding our cosmos lies not in comprehending the initiation of
its structure and organization, but rather in understanding the
laws and principles of nature that maintain the cosmic system
and cause it to operate in an orderly fashion.

But in ignoring the deeper purpose underlying each cause and
effect simply because the issue is so complex, scientists would

appear to be taking what can only be described as an easy way out. Rav Shimon Bar Yohai, in *The Zohar*, recognized that in order to face the unknowable, it is necessary for us to discover the primary cause of events—an undertaking with which contemporary science cannot cope.

Kabbalah describes the cosmos in terms of positive and negative energy-intelligence. The internal nonmaterial consciousness of celestial bodies are, like the soul of man, in direct communication with the Creator. The seven planets act as orbital channels for the seven diffused emanations of cosmic intelligence known as the seven Sfirot.

The encapsulated, intelligent coded messages of the Sfirot are the primal forces that account for our solar system as well as for the cosmos itself. What emerges from *The Zohar's* revelation is that forms of intelligence emanating from these Sfirot are directly responsible for our universal manifestation. More important, they are the forces that impel our day-to-day activities. In other words, it is unseen extraterrestrial forces that affect and determine the ups and downs of everyday phenomena.

CONSCIOUSNESS IS CONTAGIOUS

To ensure fulfillment, we must find ourselves unified with the soul consciousness of the cosmos. Yet the concept of soul consciousness extends beyond the celestial region of the planets and signs of our constellation.

We should not be surprised if computers and other high-tech mechanisms begin to exhibit their own consciousness. The designers who install computer programs and the consumers who use these machines all leave their mark on them. The closer we come to subatomic particles and atoms, the closer we are drawn to the psychology and robotic consciousness of these instruments of communication. To be sure, such instruments have no free will in and of themselves. They do, however, have an internal consciousness to perform as they have been instructed. The material, corporeal aspect of these information machines falls within the category of body consciousness. As such, they become subject to, and are influenced by, negative environments and associations. This concept has very tangible and practical effects. For example, a table in a restaurant formerly occupied by negative occupants should be avoided, as the vibrations of those former occupants perpetuate their negative influence via the body consciousness of the chairs and tables. So if you haven't enjoyed your meal at one of your favorite restaurants, it may well be the fault of the table and not the chef!

Becoming attuned to your environment is as critical as becoming familiar with the type of food you eat or the nature of the company you keep. Before moving into a new apartment or a new home, for example, we must become fully informed about its former occupants, whose vibrations will continue to make their presence felt long after they themselves have left. If misfortune or grief was the fortune of these former inhabitants, the new homeowners can expect this negative energy-intelligence to continue to exert an influence on their own lives and relationships.

A close reading of *The Zohar* suggests that inanimate objects are really not as lifeless as we once thought. The air and the earth are both made of vibrating molecules and atoms. Both consist of particles that interact with one another by creating and destroying other particles. In a similar manner, the atoms of your body collectively participate in a cosmic dance of energy and activity. Things "out there" are not independent of us. To the contrary, everyone and everything acts on and interacts with one another. Consequently, the varied soul and body consciousness of our universe combines to create and influence the activities and movements of all within it.

There would thus appear to be little room for us to act or behave in a manner that might provide for free choice and determination. This concept, in fact, underlies quantum theory and has led some scientists to conclude that man lives in a universe in which no one can actually be held responsible for his actions. After all, if outside influences are so pervasive and intense, what degree of free will does humanity have?

Stretching this idea to its extreme, a murderer or an assassin might claim, in his own defense, that forces lying beyond his control were responsible for his criminal activities. Yet despite these inferences, the revelation on Mount Sinai does indicate room for free will. The Ten Commandments, which include the prohibition of criminal activity, clearly state that there is a degree of control involved in humanity's decision-making process. Although it is true that we are continually bombarded by an infinite array of thoughts, the kabbalistic worldview is that we can and do exercise free choice.

All signposts seem to point in the same direction: Outside influences extending all the way to the farthest galaxies contribute significantly to the shaping of our behavior and our manner of doing things. There is no way in which we can just make these energy-intelligences fade away, as they are part of our universal landscape. They will either assist and support our objectives or create a chaotic environment in which things begin to go awry. Tapping the positive energy-intelligence of our cosmos or creating security shields to protect us from cosmic negative activity is what the study of Kabbalah is all about.

Because we are acutely aware of our limitations and the inherent prejudices into which we are born, our collective consciousness alone affords us very little opportunity to achieve a quantum positive attitude. But when we scan *The Zohar* and participate in kabbalistic meditation, we foster a more cosmically positive level of energy-intelligence for ourselves, the world, and the universe.

While deliberately avoiding preconceived ideas or political links, Kabbalah endeavors to promote the individual's awareness and recognition of humanity's greater potential. Studying Kabbalah will both permit and induce all of humanity to realize that whatever serves the collective consciousness of humanity also serves the needs of the individual.

INTELLIGENCE: FOR EVERY ANSWER, ANOTHER QUESTION

Man's mind has always seemed as mysterious and fascinating as the universe itself. Yet only in recent times has the investigation of the mind's nature become the domain of experimental science. And as greater insight is gained on the nature of our mental processes, more and more questions are being raised.

Intelligence is one of the most desirable of all human traits, but intelligence does not mean the same thing to everyone. Some claim it refers to an ability to perform mental functions successfully. But we would ask, "Which specific functions are considered relevant?"

Reasoning capabilities have something to do with intelligence, and memory plays a role in it as well. But what about people whose level of inventiveness is extraordinary, but whose memory fails them just when a piece of vital information is required? And what about people who supposedly belong at the other end of the spectrum, the so-called "idiot savants"? This term is used to describe individuals who find it difficult to perform everyday mental functions, but who display extraordinary capabilities in specific areas.

To this very day, intelligence tests have frustrated many psychiatrists and analysts. The concept of intelligence quotient, or IQ, is under constant revision simply because the everyday information upon which the tests rely are constantly changing. Although intelligence tests are tremendously useful and will doubtless be with us for some time, mental health experts are still not sure just what these yardsticks actually measure.

Until very recently, psychologists held the belief that intelligence was governed by heredity and consequently remained invariant throughout life. To the extent that IQ tests actually measure intelligence, however, there are strong indications that intelligence can in fact change in the course of an individual's lifetime. For instance, it has become increasingly difficult to ignore the overwhelming evidence that intelligence can be enhanced by education. Let us therefore face up to the naked truth that, for all the scientific research and data that have been accumulated over the years, we are no closer than we have ever been to a clear-cut definition of intelligence. No test yet devised can really measure raw intelligence in a manner that is not influenced by exposure to the learning process. A better-than-average performance on an IQ test may reflect nothing more than a better-than-average educational experience.

By contrast, the kabbalistic view of intelligence is completely relative to, and dependent on, each unique and particular individual. From a kabbalistic standpoint, there are no objective yardsticks with which to measure the intelligence of a human being. The most comprehensive measurements, which unfortunately are concealed, relate to one's prior incarnation. As a result of the *Tikkune* process, however, any individual, irrespective of his or her social environment, family, or other involvements, can get started on a spiral of intellectual growth.

The levels of intelligence are known by their coded kabbalistic names, which the kabbalist can clearly recognize. The Sfirot, or levels of consciousness, fall into five gradations toward which humanity can aspire to achieve higher levels of awareness and creativity. From a kabbalistic standpoint, there is no such thing as the power of the subconscious mind. To the contrary, the mind of each person provides the same ability and capabilities; it is merely a channel. Differences in the use of the mind hinge solely on our desire to grow spiritually. Psychiatrists and psychologists have mistaken the subconscious mind for the consciousness, which already exists in the cosmos. The mind is just the medium through which we connect to the varied levels of consciousness that belong to the upper realm of the cosmos.

ARE INTELLIGENCE TESTS REALLY INTELLIGENT?

Although most of us like to think we know intelligence when we see it, explaining just what intelligence involves is a problem that stubbornly persists. In truth, researchers have not yet arrived at a definition that satisfies them all. Some think of intelligence as a combination of related abilities, including insight, creativity, flexibility, and the speed with which the brain can process information.

Most intelligence tests now in use reflect this multifaceted view. Some tests measure the abilities just mentioned, while others consider additional factors, such as memory or spatial perception.

Does this sort of testing conclude that if someone cannot instantly recall information, there is a deficiency in that person's intelligence quotient? I find this very difficult to accept, given the fact that there is little consensus as to what constitutes intelligence in the first place. To assume that intelligence is purely and simply a product of genes and the environment only clouds the issue. No single gene has been positively identified as contributing to human intelligence.

Evidence that heredity plays a major role in this area comes only from studies of closely related family members. Identical twins are more alike in their intelligence quotient than are others who do not share the same genes. From a kabbalistic perspective, however, we must ask, "Why were these identical twins placed in that environment in the first place?" Simply put, we must first review the possible causes and ascertain what initiated the circumstances before examining the final outcome.

Thus, a conclusion that identical twins have similar IQs requires us to reflect on the causative factors that brought these twins into the world. Data of a physical nature can never explain first causes or serve as a basis for ultimate conclusions. A starting point for any investigation requires, above all, answers to the "why" of things. Thus, the first question the researcher must ask is, "Why were these identical twins, and not some other pair of twins, brought into the world by these specific parents?" To find the answer, we must look toward patterns of reincarnation and the *Tikkune* process.

Kabbalah teaches that the true definition of intelligence lies in the accumulation of metaphysical "data" derived from the experience and environment of all our former lifetimes. Present intelligence is the mental computer printout of these former lifetimes. With this understanding, let us turn again to the question of whether we can raise our IQ. Studies of deliberate efforts to raise IQ are almost nonexistent. The reason for this lack of interest lies in the fact that most researchers have already accepted the acknowledged role of heredity in determining intelligence. They have concluded that after the age of seven, a person's IQ tends to stay about the same, with the implication that raising one's IQ is virtually impossible.

But does this statement not imply that all our activities in adulthood should remain at the elementary school level? Furthermore, a tendency to retain the same IQ throughout our lives again suggests the existence of an immutable "fate" upon which free will can exert no effect. Once again, this relegates humanity to mere robotic consciousness.

The ongoing discussion of determinism versus free will is one that we laypeople must begin to understand and resolve. What's more, we very much want to understand it. People all around the globe are interested in change. People want to take matters into their own hands rather than leave it to government or to other social agencies. In a sense, this is a very encouraging sign. It means that the "man in the street" has come to realize that his future health and welfare depend more and more on his personal decisions and lifestyle choices.

We now return to our original question, "Can we raise our IQ?" The answer is clearly affirmative. The inner Light of mind consists of, and remains bound up with, the *Tikkune* process.

Whenever we achieve a spiritual correction through Restriction, we remove a barrier or curtain that has separated us from our inner Light. At any given moment in our present lifetime, when the opportunity for Restriction presents itself and we succeed in our correction, the removal of the barrier will reveal a higher level of consciousness and intelligence in our particular inner Light.

Intelligence, as defined by the kabbalist, is our "limited" aggregate or universal capacity to think, act, and deal effectively in our corporeal realm. The intelligence of each person must be considered to be limited simply because the ability and capacity to receive are governed by the individual soul consciousness prescribed for that individual's *Tikkune* process. Consequently, each of us must of necessity enter this world with an inner Light that provides the minimum energy of intelligence we need to deal properly with the movie of our *Tikkune* process. There is never a time when the inner Light intelligence is inadequate to the task of coping with an impending *Tikkune*—that is, the correction of a situation that one failed to correct in a previous lifetime. And with each successful encounter—wherein Restriction became the overpowering activity "this time around"—the individual is rewarded with an elevated state of consciousness over and above the original inner Light intelligence with which he or she was born.

If, for example, a man committed a particular crime on a certain day of his 20th year in one or more prior lifetimes, the opportunity for correction will present itself again on that same day in his present 20th year. If the man exercises Restriction this time, the curtain that veiled the inner Light consciousness will be removed. By virtue of this Restriction, a higher level of intelligence will be achieved.

So the "exceptional cases" noted in many studies that suggest the possibility of raising the IQ are not really exceptional at all. To the contrary, they represent examples of people who have demonstrated Restriction in their lives and have thereby revealed a higher level of intelligence. Throughout humankind, the potential for these higher levels exists from the moment of our birth. We all possess a gold mine from which we can extract everything we need to live joyously and abundantly!

INNER LIGHT CONSCIOUSNESS

During the late 20th century, Western civilization seemed ready to surrender everything to the pursuit of personal pleasures. Restriction was uncommon, misunderstood, and all but forgotten. The destruction of the earth's natural resources continued unabated, with no regard to the price that would ultimately be paid for such extravagance. Values eroded, especially for human life.

The early years of the 21st century, on the other hand, have brought us to the realization that it is futile to attempt to solve society's problems by addressing such manifestations as wages, housing, illness, and crime. At least this is the perception of the general public. The institutions of society, however, continue to lag behind, with government, business, and medicine continuing to focus on symptoms rather than on causes. The main flaw in this perspective lies in its failure to ask the question "why?" Rather than focusing energy on curing the entity as a whole, attention is directed toward an endless patchwork process in which the outward signs are treated while the metaphysical cause is neglected.

Inner Light exists within the confines of the metaphysical level. kabbalists have long understood that to solve any problem, we must first see that problem in the context of a greater whole. In order to comprehend the microcosm, it is necessary for us to consider the macrocosm. Yet the rewards of this understanding have been and continue to be withheld from the general population.

From a kabbalistic standpoint, there is no hidden power of the subconscious mind. Many spiritually oriented people around the world have already begun their journey in acquiring the infinite intelligence that all of us can possess. And by spiritually oriented, I mean those people who have come to the realization that they must strive toward a sharing consciousness and introduce the principle of Restriction into their lives on a daily basis. They are in control of this process. They are not subject to the constraints of the unconscious mind. Indeed, the infinite intelligence of the cosmos -- which is unhindered by time, space, and motion—can reveal everything we need to know at every moment, provided that we are open-minded and receptive to it.

We can draw on the awesome power of the cosmos at will, thereby increasing our consciousness and awareness beyond our wildest imaginations. By learning how to tap and reveal the hidden power of the cosmos, we can bring more power and wealth into our lives as well as more joy, happiness, and health. This vast reservoir of cosmic beneficence belongs to all of us. However, only those who gain the necessary knowledge and understanding with which to expand the capacity of their mind power can be the recipients of this infinite source of wisdom. It is our right and privilege to discover this inner world of consciousness. Although invisible, its forces are awesome and mighty. They can enable us to find the solution for every problem and, more significantly, to find the original cause of every effect.

In each and every human being there is but one mind. However, the mind possesses two functional sets of consciousness. These two functions are directly connected with the kabbalistic doctrines of inner Light consciousness and encircling Light consciousness.

Inner Light consciousness includes both the rational, conscious mind and the unconscious mind. Conscious awareness is an automatic process of the physical brain. Although scientists claim there is a relationship between consciousness and the brain, they really do not know what that relationship is. For the present, what might be considered mind consciousness falls within the category of inner Light consciousness.

Scientists have long avoided the idea that any rational intellect might exist below conscious awareness. Psychosomatic or emotional problems, or worrying without reason, are some of the behavioral consequences of abnormal mental activity that produce stressful subconscious struggles. The role of the unconscious in emotional disorders is rarely mentioned by psychiatrists despite the mind's unique ability to form abstract concepts or images that can actually engender physical change in the body.

Conscious and unconscious realities are unique and individual. They are established within each person at a level of intelligence that depends entirely on the dictates of previous lifetimes. To a certain extent, these levels can be measured. The origins of human behavior can be traced to prior incarnations and are not affected by the circumstances of human environments.

The mind is nonmaterial—a unique, intangible product of our prior lifetimes that processes the information fed to it by our surroundings. The mind then releases its findings to the brain. In this way, the mind possesses the ability to regulate and control the brain.

The brain as a product of mind activity controls the electrical and chemical functions of the body. The brain, according to kabbalistic teachings, is the *Keter* (Crown), or seed. of all physical manifestation and activity. A kabbalist always seeks first causes. The head is the *Keter* of human development; it grows first and most rapidly in the mother's womb. Its internal energy-intelligence consists of the *Sfirah Keter*, which has the awesome power of all-inclusiveness. Like the seed of a tree, which includes and encompasses all future physical manifestations, the brain thus possesses the awesome power to control and regulate the distribution of the mind power produced by the mental computer printout.

It is beyond our ability to comprehend the awesome power of the mind as it directs the electrochemical processes of the human body with such precision. In some way the mind establishes goals with which to accomplish a specific assignment. By controlling particular physiological activities, the mind even projects the results of what is to be achieved in the process. Indeed, according to kabbalistic teachings, the task to be accomplished has already been established long before the elements of the brain are called upon to perform the functions necessary to carry out the mind's intention.

An idea that has been grasped by the mind already includes that which must be accomplished to meet its objective, as well as the intentions and decisions with which to control the neurophysiologic processes needed to achieve its goal. To appreciate this extraordinary power of the mind, we need only consider the enormous amount of advance information provided by the mind's former incarnations. Because of the mind's built-in "robotic consciousness," flaws or mistakes in relaying instructions to the brain are nonexistent. The brain's function is one of executing the intentions and decisions of the mind at the physical level.

Abstract thought, advanced reasoning, learning, judgment, planning—none of these would be possible without the highly developed human mind. But the mind is much more than just an energy center of intellectual activity. The mind also regulates, directs, and coordinates all the sensory impressions we receive and all the emotions we feel. Because of our individual *Tikkune* process, which is bound up with our prior lifetimes, we can gain insight into why each of us views the same things somewhat differently. We can understand why we react in different ways to the same circumstances. In short, our individual *Tikkune* process is what differentiates one human being from another.

WHAT'S PLAYING?

I have compared the mind and brain to a film projector. Just as what comes out of a projector depends on what film has been loaded into it, so too does the mind-brain follow the instructions of the *Tikkune* process "movie." But it is there that all comparison with a computer ends. Whereas a film projector reveals visual information one frame at a time, the brain—with its trillions of cross-linked neural connections—processes information along millions of multidirectional pathways all at the same instant. A projector cannot decide that it is wasting its talents or that it should embark on a new way of life. Even a state-of-the-art computer cannot dramatically alter its own program. The human brain, however, must always reprogram itself before moving in a new direction.

The brain—the command station of the nervous system—also mediates the intrinsic ability of the human mind to exercise free will. The *Tikkune* process permits each person to alter his or her mind program and thus bring about changes in the ultimate manifestation of the brain's activities.

The mind and its link to the human body—including the brain—remain mysterious. The great gap that science must bridge in the knowledge of the mind can be expressed as follows: "How are the actions of the nervous system translated into consciousness? What role does the brain play in this scenario?" As new knowledge is uncovered, science is making amendments and replacing outmoded points of view. The result, however, is only the creation of more and more complicated questions that leave unresolved the key question, "What is the mind?"

The brain serves a twofold purpose. Its first purpose is to project the image of its mental feature film. The second is to manifest the instructions and regulate its dynamic movement within the physical body. Science, as we have discussed, has proposed a complete division between mind and body. Of course, once the inclusive nature of the mind was acknowledged, a host of new problems arose, many of which remain unanswered to this day.

If the mind is accepted as the knower of all the enormously complex matters and relationships of life, we might ask, "How does the mind know this and relate to it?" The brain was and is seen by many as a mere warehouse stuffed with all kinds of furniture. In this view, intuition, déjà vu, flashes of creativity, and everything we know about the world around us must be accounted for as something that was "brought in from outside." The hardheaded realists, known as empiricists, refuse to acknowledge the concept of innate ideas. They refuse to accept the idea of a brain born with a small but basic supply of furniture—inner Light—despite overwhelming evidence supporting it.

The mysterious realm of the unconscious is, Kabbalistically speaking, our mental movie, as produced and cast by our former lifetimes and prior incarnations. The complex machinations of the brain provide a glimpse into our own metaphysical production company. To appreciate the vastness of the mind that will eternally remain concealed from any physical mode of detection, let us briefly glance at the awesome complexity of the human nervous system.

Complete networks of nerve cells run throughout the body, connecting every bit of tissue with the more than 10 billion nerve cells of the governing brain. Electrical impulses travel along these neuronal superhighways, connecting the infrastructure at speeds of up to 400 miles per hour. These impulses perform incredible leaping feats across the narrow gaps that exist between cells. Together, the elements of this communication system far outperform any high-tech telecommunication system designed by man. The various networks simultaneously perform a dazzling array of tasks.

Whatever the nature of the mind or our mental computer, the mechanisms through which the mind expresses itself are beyond scientific belief. Consequently, when considering the mind itself, where and from which point can scientists begin their investigation or research? Scientists face insurmountable obstacles even in dealing with the physical brain alone. Therefore, examination of the mental process, or of how the mind functions, is a study that has no starting point. The dilemma faced by psychiatrists and other researchers continues unabated. Today, there is hardly a respectable neuroscientist who thinks that the mind exists apart from the functions of the physical brain and body. Yet what some researchers have called the "ghost in the machine" continues to haunt efforts to scientifically describe human conscious and unconscious thinking. The answers lie unmistakably in the realm of metaphysics—the reality level in which the biochemical model reaches an abrupt end.

SLEEP: MORE THAN YOU EVER DREAMED

On average, we spend almost a third of our lives in sleep. Yet we know little about precisely what sleep is supposed to accomplish. Some researchers believe that sleep serves some restorative function. Our bodies require sleep, but how does sleep fulfill these necessities? Why do we awaken refreshed? To this day, the answers to these questions remain unclear.

Science knows little of the night life of the brain. Only in the 1950s did investigators at the University of Chicago find that sleepers periodically produce rapid eye movements. When these subjects were awakened during such movements, they testified that they had been dreaming. Researchers also determined that the heartbeat quickens during dreams and that brain-wave patterns resemble those of someone who is awake and alert. Quite an active night life for the brain, whose enormous and complex activity never permits it the luxury of a vacation or even a day's rest!

With all this activity, combined with the many chores the brain must regulate, control, and initiate even while sleeping, it is little wonder that our mental institutions are filled to capacity. The sleep phenomenon, coupled with all the mysteries that surround it, establishes conclusively that there does indeed exist a "ghost in the brain machine." That ghost is our inner Light—the mind, our mental computer. There is no other answer that can explain the awesome capacity of the brain to perform 24 hours a day for years on end.

Although there are many similarities in the way electronic machines and the brain function, no one has yet come forward with a claim that the performance of a man-made machine will some day equal that of the brain. Both the brain and a computer process incoming raw material with the support of complex circuitry. Both demonstrate built-in systems for storing enormous quantities of information in their memory banks. However, the brain calls upon stored-up information that it has not even experienced before—at least not in this lifetime. The computer, on the other hand, can access only stored information that has been placed there by a programmer or program.

Prolonged lack of sleep results in an inability to function as usual. We suddenly find ourselves in a condition in which we have difficulty carrying out basic mental and physical chores. Sleep deprivation experiments reveal that a person may experience extreme vulnerability with lack of sleep. He or she may even hallucinate and exhibit other signs of mental illness. Why do people who have trouble sleeping suffer a multitude of emotional and physical ailments, in addition to feeling constantly fatigued, despite their lying in bed and resting for days on end? There is no long-term chemical solution for this difficulty. In fact, sleeping pills actually make insomnia worse rather than better. There is no such thing as a pill that can foster normal sleep.

But let us now return to our original question, "Why is sleep necessary?" According to *The Zohar*, sleep greatly benefits and improves an individual's physical and mental well-being, thereby helping achieve Kabbalah's essential objective of joy and fulfillment.

The Zohar tells us that during sleep,

> . . . the soul mounts up, returning to its source, while the body is still as a stone, thus reverting to its own origin. While in that state, the body is beset by the influences of the dark side, with the result that its hands become defiled and remain so until they are washed in the morning. As for the soul, it is absorbed within the all-embracing unified whole of the Creator. The soul then re-emerges—that is to say, it is born anew, as fresh and new as at its former birth. This is the secret meaning of the words, "They are new every morning; great is thy thoughtfulness."

The soul, states *The Zohar*, requires a "pause that refreshes." Following its daily battle with the body, its adversary and opponent, the soul requires an infusion of energy in order to continue its struggle with body consciousness until life's end. Soul consciousness is one of a Desire to Receive for the Purpose of Sharing. By contrast, body consciousness pursues the indulgence of a Desire to Receive for Oneself Alone. The battle goes on and on, with both sides paying a heavy price. The soul sees itself as the enemy of the body, and this is by no means an inaccurate view. The aim of body consciousness, after all, is to prevent the soul from achieving its *Tikkune*, or correction. However, the body does provide the soul with the opportunity to complete its *Tikkune*. Without body consciousness, the idea of free will is not a reality.

Sleep, then, is a necessary function for the soul, and the need for it is compelling. By falling into a natural state in which conscious activity is suspended, the soul has the opportunity to recharge. Body consciousness is like a parasite, snatching whatever energy it can from its enemy, the soul. The soul's only reprieve, as *The Zohar* beautifully states, is to become "absorbed within the all-embracing unified whole of the Light."

SLEEP AND IMMUNITY

The physical body and body consciousness are two distinct concepts. The former does not require rest or sleep. Evidence of this lies in the 24 hour activity of our body. The heart performs throughout the day; heaven help us if it did not. The brain is just as active during sleep as it is when we are awake, consuming 20% of the oxygen that our breathing takes in. Body consciousness, however, behaves very differently. Our Desire to Receive for Ourselves Alone "lies still as a stone" while we are asleep. This is necessary in order to permit the soul to rejuvenate itself.

In essence, the phenomenon of sleep centers on the ability to shut down, for a time, the internal energy-intelligence of body consciousness. The body as a whole was created with inner healing powers. The human immune system has a highly impressive arsenal with which to ward off disease. Provided that the system is healthy and strong enough, our natural antibodies overwhelm any invaders. A major problem of modern medicine, however, lies in the fact that drugs and other therapies act as substitutes for the body's natural healing powers. Antibiotics may kill useful and beneficial bacteria as well as those that cause disease. Modern medicine, in short, has interposed its own system of defense, bypassing the healing powers that are an inherent part of the human body. Even the finest, most dedicated medical practitioner can never think or act with the sophistication and sensitivity of our own natural immune system. When our medical needs require a particular chemical, our inner healing system provides us with the precise requirement, where and when we need it.

ROBOTIC CONSCIOUSNESS, SOUL CONSCIOUSNESS

The 19th century English poet John Keats ended his famous poem about listening to a nightingale with an inquiry into the ambiguity of consciousness. Was Keats really hearing the bird's song, or was he dreaming of hearing it? How can we know the difference? The truth is, most of us are sound asleep even when we think we are wide awake—because we are not aware of the wellspring of infinite intelligence that lies dormant within us. The teachings of Kabbalah can provide a link to the hidden power of our subconscious mental computer. We do not have to acquire this power; we already possess it. Within the depths of our soul consciousness lies an infinite supply of all that is necessary for our physical, emotional, and spiritual well-being. In the wisdom of the subconscious mind, we can find the solutions for every problem. Once access to this realm has become an accomplished fact, our conscious state can no longer be interfered with by body consciousness, with its fragmented, distorted influence.

To remove confusion and limitations once and for all, we must remove the cause—and the cause is the content of our conscious minds. In other words, the way we think is the way we act. The shepherd must lead the flock, and not the other way around. The conscious mind must be made subject to the authority of the subconscious soul consciousness. When the conscious mind is overcome with worry and anxiety, the negative emotions that result must be reversed. The effects of this reversal will be truly revolutionary, because soul consciousness knows nothing of chaos, disorder, misfortune, and their related negative effects. Rather, soul consciousness is the channel for, and the expression of, the all-embracing Light. Soul consciousness is the seed and foundation of our being, and as such it is infinitely more powerful than body consciousness, which by comparison is nothing but a superficial presence and influence in our lives.

For the present, however, it may certainly appear that body consciousness is firmly in control. Considering the destructive (and self-destructive) behavior of humankind, body consciousness seems to enjoy an undisputed, unopposed conquest of every aspect of human existence. In opposition to this, kabbalistic teachings powerfully support the endeavor to end human carnage and suffering. How does this support express itself? By connecting us with the awesome omnipotent Light that governs all things—including body consciousness itself.

As we look around us, we surely must notice that the vast majority of individuals live in a world of robotic consciousness, seemingly beyond the control of any individual or even the collective human race. Little wonder that economic misfortune and degenerative diseases are the continuing curses of our civilization! Whereas our body consciousness is a connection to limitation and fragmentation, our subconscious soul consciousness is an extension of the infinite Light. Inasmuch as soul consciousness speaks to us in the form of intuitions, creative ideas, and the urge to share, it is not surprising that writers, musicians, and other artists are particularly in tune with their subconscious mental powers. These are the true source of artistic inspiration. Mark Twain, for example, remarked on many occasions that he never really worked a day in his life. All his writings and all his wit and humor were the result of his tapping of the inexhaustible reservoir of his subconscious mind. I am certain that every great artist would have understood exactly what Twain meant and would have concurred.

KNOWING THE LIGHT

The spiritual essence of the Hebrew alphabet—the Aleph Beth—emanates from the highest realms of energy-intelligence. The Aleph Beth is permeated by the Light of the Creator and is also sealed with the Impression of His Signature, which is Truth.

Who is close to the Light of the Creator? This question is posed in *The Zohar* with regard to the words of scripture: "The Lord is near to all those who call upon Him, to all those who call upon (to connect with) Me in Truth."

The Zohar then asks, "Is there anyone who would call falsely?" And it continues, "Rav Abba said, 'Yes. It is the one who calls and knows not Whom he calls.'"

This brings us to the question, "Why is knowing the Light essential to connection?" *The Zohar* emphasizes the negative consequence of not knowing, which is the withdrawal of the Light from our being and from our consciousness. When we attempt to discuss a connection with any kind of metaphysical power source, a basic understanding of the source and the receiver must first be in place. An understanding of fundamental metaphysics is an integral part of communication, without which true connection can never materialize.

It is written in the Book of Genesis, "And Adam knew Eve, his wife; and she conceived, and bore Cain." According to *The Zohar*, the use of the word "knew" refers to sexual intercourse. But this word raises many questions.

Why does the verse use the word "knew," which normally denotes an intellectual process, to describe the physical act of sexual connection? What is the real meaning of this coded message? Why this word, when similar Hebrew words would have explained the passage more explicitly?

As *The Zohar* explains, in this profound verse we discover a "true connection" with metaphysical forces that is dependent on the knowledge derived from the establishment of proper channels. Knowledge is an integral part of this communication system because without it, any system is ineffective. Thus, when Adam "knew" Eve, he established a method of clear communication through which metaphysical energy could flow unimpeded. This is made absolutely clear by *The Zohar*, which states that "true connection" with the Light is essential for the realization of any objective. Knowledge, then, is a fundamental means of connecting with the Light.

There is yet another facet, states *The Zohar*, that is included in the basic concept of truth. Throughout history, the desire to act in the "name of the Lord" has brought forth centuries of murder and suffering. All religions portray themselves as defenders of the Light. How, then, asks *the Zohar*, can we determine whether or not our perspective is bound up and connected with truth? How can we know whether we are "calling with the seal of the King"? The seal, with the Impression of His Signature, is a code for the Central Column, which balances everything. So it is stated in the Scriptures: "For He gives the power of truth to Jacob (representing the Central Column, which is balance) and the power of mercy (representing the Right Column, which is positive energy) to Abraham." Therefore it is written:

> The Lord is close to those who call upon Him in truth. And those who do not know to call upon Him, the Lord withdraws from them.

CHAPTER FIVE:
HEALTH AND HEALING

WHAT DOES HEALING MEAN?

Today more than ever, our society has become deeply concerned with addressing the fundamental issues of illness and wellness. Health care costs have risen to a point at which fewer and fewer people can afford even to contemplate the possibility of getting sick. The fear of illness, and concern with how to heal it, are on everyone's mind. Yet rarely do we ask, "What does healing really mean? Where does healing power come from?"

It would be reassuring to think that this power resides in our physicians and surgeons. The truth, however, is that no physician has ever "healed" even a single patient. What really happens in medicine is something quite different. The real mission and expertise of doctors lie in creating an environment in which the natural healing process can take place. Medicine removes blockages or barriers in a patient. A surgeon who removes a physical impairment has done nothing more than that, nor has a physician who reduces a debilitating symptom such as fever, inflammation, or swelling.

The interaction between the physical body and our two states of consciousness—soul consciousness and body consciousness—determines the state of our physical health. Whenever soul consciousness prevails and dominates body consciousness, we are in tune with the intrinsic principle of harmony and continuity. Fortunately, most children born into this world are perfectly healthy, with all their organs functioning in an excellent manner. We should be capable of maintaining this normal state and remain healthy, strong individuals throughout the course of our lives.

In this sense, illness should be understood as fundamentally opposed to natural processes. By this I mean that illness runs counter to the stream of soul consciousness, which is the most authentic aspect of ourselves. When we act and think negatively, illness arises because we have become drawn into the abyss of our body consciousness. There is a very basic law of life: If we entertain thoughts and activities that are not in accordance with the soul–consciousness principle of "love thy neighbor," these thoughts and activities will eventually bring about disease in the body and misfortune in other areas of our lives.

If, by contrast, we are in harmony with our soul consciousness, we increase the input and distribution of the vital life forces of our soul consciousness throughout our being. The study of Kabbalah provides this vital connection. It helps eliminate our thoughts of fear, jealousy, hatred, and anxiety as well as those negative activities which break down and destroy the immune system, causing nerves and glands to be impaired and resulting in an overall degeneration of our vital organs.

We are the captains of our soul consciousness, and we are the masters of our fate. Free will is ours. But at any time, our *Tikkune* process may place us in an arena in which our free will encounters our destiny. At any given moment, we may be called upon to decide whether to exercise Restriction or to respond with a negative action.

If restraint is our chosen course of action, then we have, for that particular *Tikkune* process, removed ourselves from the vulnerability of becoming influenced by our body consciousness. We have shut the door to, and eliminated the consequences of, body-consciousness domination. At that point, we have in effect produced a new movie—one in which soul consciousness is permitted to restore the normal functions of the body and to bring joy and fulfillment into our lives.

In truth, the healing process is the life force within our soul consciousness. When the barriers that inhibit and obstruct the flow of the life-force energy are removed, healing takes place as a natural process. The potential for these inner obstacles comes into being upon the origin of body consciousness; the opportune time for them to become activated is when a failure in the *Tikkune* process has taken place. The influence of body consciousness then invades our being through the opening that we ourselves have created with our negative thoughts and actions.

Kabbalah will always support us in restoring the powers of our soul consciousness. By studying Kabbalah, we can truly heal ourselves. The degree of our healing, however, depends on our ability to restore our individual inner Light to its fullest power and revelation.

Each step in life's journey represents another step, either forward or backward, in the *Tikkune* process. As we have discussed (and regardless of what academic researchers may tell us), opportunities abound for increasing our intelligence, provided that we create this increase within the framework of our spiritual correction. In a similar manner, healing is always possible once we move forward with the essential task of our lives, which is our *Tikkune*.

Throughout the ages, people of all nations and cultures believed that there resided within some individuals a healing power that could restore health. This capability for healing the sick was said to be possessed by the High Priest and other holy men. Indeed, the "laying on of hands" has long been recognized by kabbalists as a channel for the transference of energy. At the same time, however, Kabbalah teaches that no one beyond ourselves is needed in order for the restoration of health to occur. We can become our own healers. The Light Force will flow instantly through us if only we permit it to do so. Of course, we can make the self-destructive choice of interfering with the normal, healthy rhythm of bodily functions, such as those of the heart, lungs, liver, and other vital organs. This can take place not only when we eat unhealthy foods, take drugs, or smoke cigarettes, but also when we allow our lives to become dominated by the Desire to Receive for Ourselves Alone. Therefore, we must carefully watch our thoughts and actions, especially our dealings with other people. "Do not do unto others what you would not have others do unto you" is more than just an aphorism. It is the key to health and healing at the most fundamental level of our lives.

"PRIMITIVE" MEDICINE

The interest in achieving greater individual control over our lives and destinies has recently become more pronounced among some medical professionals. Some within the medical community have even begun to recognize that so-called primitive medicine sometimes achieves remarkable cures with just a few herbs administered in ceremonial fashion. How is this possible? It's because the rituals involving these herbs were designed to arouse the individual consciousness and to strengthen people's belief both in themselves and in their connection with a higher power. All of this is based on knowledge that, in the final analysis, it is the patient himself who brings about healing.

In the March 1989 issue of the prestigious British medical journal The Lancet, a detailed study on the survival of breast cancer patients was presented. This study showed that 80 percent of patients described as having a "fighting spirit" achieved a ten-year survival rate, whereas only 20% of those identified as "feeling helpless" survived for ten years. This report underscores a dilemma that persists in modern medicine to this day—that we do not foster the patient's natural healing powers. Unfortunately, there is no required coursework in medical school on how to encourage patients' ability to heal themselves. Instead, patients are expected to submit passively to the directives of the medical establishment. Yet at Johns Hopkins Hospital in Baltimore, Maryland, breast cancer patients who were considered "nonconformists" and were judged to have "poor relationships" with their physicians were found to have longer-term survival rates. Simply put, patients who were assertive and shared responsibility for their recovery, although considered "bad" patients, achieved better results. For such patients, the response to a doctor who claimed that he was the captain of the ship was, "I'm not sure I want to board!"

Change is definitely coming in this arena. Surgeons no longer freely assault and invade our bodies at will. Oncologists will not poison people to kill disease but will instead take into consideration patients' abilities to heal themselves. And the transition is coming more swiftly than any scientist currently imagines.

COSMIC ZONES

A major cause of breakdown or damage to the immune system stems from exposure to various negative cosmic danger zones. The responsibility for avoiding these zones rests with all of us, and ignorance of these devastating cosmic events will not prevent their invasion of a healthy body. Zoharic teachings reveal that cosmic predisposition can play a role in a long list of illnesses. Kabbalists are able to zero in on these cosmic markers in order to map their locations and time frames.

The use of such markers to predict disease is enhanced by data extracted from the world's largest and most comprehensive collection of metaphysical knowledge, which includes the *Book of Formation*, *The Zohar*, and the writings of Rav Isaac Luria. I have no doubt that these kabbalistic tools will someday be used to predict an individual's vulnerability to disease from the moment of conception—and that science will in time be able to validate such findings.

The idea that our bodies and vital organs are bound up and connected with cosmic zones is clearly stated in *The Zohar*, and knowledge of this connection represents a major step toward control over our bodies, especially over illness when it strikes. It is therefore in our best interests to understand this aspect of the teachings of *The Zohar*. At the same time, we must become aware of those individuals who continue to lead us astray by shunning *The Zohar*'s teachings, or by claiming that *The Zohar* should be available only to a select few. As it is written:

> And Lillith is called spleen, and she goes to play with the children, later killing them, and makes of them anger and tears, to bewail them. The spleen goes to the right of the liver, which is the Angel of Death. This was created on the second day of the Work of Creation, while the other, that is the spleen, was created on the fourth day of the Work of Creation. And for this reason it is not a good omen to commence something on Mondays (the second day of the week or on Wednesdays, the fourth day of the week). Liver is death for adults; spleen is death for children!

In the foregoing *Zohar* passage, we glimpse the intimate relationship between cosmic time zones and our bodies. Yet little awareness of these zones can be found among scientists or the public at large, particularly with respect to the threat they pose to our mental and physical well-being. On the other hand, the Book of Formation, whose authorship is attributed to Abraham the Patriarch, abounds with insights on the body-cosmos connection.

I am aware, of course, that some may find this subject challenging or even alarming, suggesting as it does that everything having to do with current medical procedures must be carefully examined and possibly modified. We cannot, however, ignore the fact that what happens at birth may well pave the way for vulnerability in later life. Nor can we turn away from the realization that the movie that was shot in a past lifetime is now being projected onto the screen of our current existence.

THE MIND-BODY PROBLEM

Because of the difficulty it has in acknowledging the nonmaterial aspects of health and illness, the medical profession cannot bring itself to face the real effects of its own influence. Failure to recognize the mind-body connection in a chronic, degenerative disease such as cancer leads physicians to accept these afflictions as consequences of an inevitable deterioration of over time. This is essentially a Cartesian point of view, derived from the work of Rene Descartes, the 17th century French mathematician and philosopher.

Descartes introduced the concept of an absolute separation between mind and body. In the Cartesian view, the body was to be understood completely in terms of the arrangement and function of various parts, as though it were no different from a well-engineered, complex machine. In a healthy person, all the parts were considered to be operational, whereas in a sick person, one or more parts were judged to be functioning improperly. Since the time of Descartes, medicine has limited its understanding of illness to the physical mechanisms involved in disease. This approach has ignored any influences of a metaphysical, noncorporeal nature on biological processes. And its effect has been to give the physician full power to invade the malfunctioning part, either surgically or chemically, in order to correct the specific malfunction.

Three centuries after Descartes, the view of the body as nothing more than a machine, of disease as a consequence of the breakdown of this machine, and of the doctor as a "Mister fix-it" remains the dominant perspective. It is no wonder that the present system of medical care now produces some physicians who are very caring individuals and others who care very little. The proportion of both types is governed simply by statistical probability. In the same way, certain hospitals are authentic places of healing, while others treat patients in a degrading and insensitive manner. All this is nothing more than the logical consequence of perceiving the body as a machine.

Humanity's finite aspect, the one percent reality, is subject to fragmented, crisis-ridden Cartesian rules and regulations. Kabbalah puts us in contact with the 99% reality that operates beyond physical limits. Only the finite reality is subject to pain and chaos. Only the infinite reality is characterized by certainty, happiness, and freedom from all pain and suffering.

THE SEARCH FOR MIND
(IN ALL THE WRONG PLACES)

In the kabbalistic view, the body is in no sense a machine. The physical matter of our body structure comprises only one percent of the space we inhabit; therefore we are 99% metaphysical beings of thought, feeling, and consciousness. By concentrating on smaller and smaller fragments of the one percent reality, science—and medicine in particular—inevitably loses sight of the patient as a human being. Although every medical researcher and physician knows anecdotally that mind and heart are essential aspects of illness and healing, this truth continues to be rejected outright by the scientific and medical establishment as a whole.

The reason for this rejection is simple, and it derives from the Cartesian hypothesis that what cannot be seen cannot be real. Since Western scientists have no idea what or where the mind is, they cannot acknowledge its reality. What they cannot squeeze into a test tube or scan with a mass spectrometer simply does not exist for them.

Regarding this subject, I am reminded of the disagreement that took place between Albert Einstein and Niels Bohr, one of the early proponents of quantum theory. When Einstein refused to accept some of the inevitable conclusions of Bohr's work, he sought support in religious terminology, as evidenced by his famous declaration, "I cannot believe that the Lord plays dice with the universe." Einstein, who since the age of 12 had rejected the concept of "Lord," now called upon that very idea—but he did so with closed eyes in order to avoid the whole truth. Einstein resorted to religious ideas out of frustration or even desperation, but he had not really integrated them into his thinking, just as he had not been able to integrate relativity with quantum theory.

To truly integrate the power of mind into the theory and practice of medicine, science will have to completely transform its narrow view of health and illness. Does this necessarily mean that science must embrace anything that is not truly "scientific?" The answer, absolutely, is no. But science will have to broaden its conceptual base to include phenomena that are real and correct despite the fact that they cannot yet be empirically verified or quantified.

A FALSE DISTINCTION

The history of modern medical science graphically illustrates the consequences of reducing our view of human life to test tubes and molecular phenomena. One of these consequences has been the splitting of the medical profession into two separate and distinct groups. Specifically, physicians are concerned with the treatment of the material body, while psychiatrists—despite the fact that they are also physicians—deal exclusively with the mind. For me, this schism clearly illustrates the difficulties that prevent medical researchers from examining the vital role of stress in illness. The study of stress has generally been confined to the psychological aspects of illness, despite the overwhelming evidence that links stress to a wide range of diseases and disorders. We will have much more to say about this in a later chapter.

To further obscure the relationship between mental health and physical well-being, psychiatrists are now treating mental illness by physical means. Specifically, they are attempting to understand mental illness in terms of physical, chemical functions in the brain. Yet the number of patients in treatment for mental illness of all kinds has not diminished but has instead increased.

The effect of cosmic influences on every human being compounds the problems the medical profession faces. As yet, nothing on this subject has even been intimated by medical researchers. Indeed, the truth of the "cosmic connection" idea will be long in coming if mental illness comes to be perceived as yet another malfunction to be treated through chemical means.

This brings to mind the story of a patient who was in a constant state of fatigue and just "not feeling good." After extensive medical testing, the patient was told that he had a clean bill of health. Objectively, he was healthy; subjectively, he felt terrible—but the very acceptance of these states as two separate categories is where the error lay. Kabbalah teaches, and has always taught, that thought controls all manifested states of physical reality. The fact that all humanity has not been educated to this truth is both a mystery and a tragedy. Just imagine the state of Oneness with the Light that would exist in the world if this knowledge were authentically embraced!

THE POWER OF DETACHMENT

Although the concept of mind over matter is dealt with only superficially in contemporary thought, *The Zohar* refers us to an important biblical text pertaining to astral influences. When Abram (later named Abraham), the first astrologer, gazed up at the stars, he foresaw that he would not have children with Sarai (later named Sarah). So the Lord told Abram not to gaze any longer into the stars. By detaching himself from the energy-intelligence of the material dimension, represented here by the stars, Abram would be able to father a son. It was simply a matter of connecting to the upper realm of consciousness.

As is always the case in the coded text of the Bible, the central message of this episode is concealed in its abstruse wording. This sometimes leaves us with the impression that the Bible merely consists of a new religion for the Israelites, together with a collection of rules for daily conduct and holiday rituals. Kabbalah, however, teaches us that we must always be wary of appearances. Things in the physical world are never what they seem, and this includes the meaning of biblical text. The physical universe can give every impression of being in a state of perpetual darkness and chaos. Yet the Light of the Creator is always present—albeit so obscured by the negative, material trappings of finite existence that a sensitive eye and a compassionate soul are required to perceive it. Is it not ironic that technological advances may ultimately provide the means by which humanity as a whole will come to recognize this truth? Whereas a strand of fiberoptic cable once carried 400 conversations, today a strand no wider than a human hair can carry many hundreds of thousands. From a kabbalistic perspective, the importance of these new technological developments lies in the fact that they may provide a conceptual framework—or a jumping-off point—that will allow humanity to place less emphasis on the material world and to connect with the 99% realm of thought energy-intelligence.

METAPHYSICS AND MEMORY

But what about the reality of pain, cancer, and other terminal diseases? Are they not real? How are we to accept these material concepts within a framework of illusion? How do we go about informing a loved one that little time remains before death? How can we minimize or even remove the scourge of pain and suffering that has become a common occurrence in our experience of reality? I can assure you that this book will not ignore these hard questions or their significance. As a starting point in this exploration, remember the old saying, "It is all in the mind." Metaphysical connections, after all, are by their very nature invisible. As a result, most of humanity is simply ignorant of them.

Even brief encounters with other dimensions provide ample evidence of a world so superior to this phase of existence that comparison is scarcely possible. Having no words to describe our metaphysical experiences—and no validation by our present culture of the existence of higher realms—we banish the memories of our extraterrestrial sojourns to hidden catacombs deep within our subconscious minds.

I have devoted these pages to making a distinction between material illusion and metaphysical reality in order to clarify a basic truth: For the most part, scientist and layman alike operate via robotic consciousness. Both have chosen to see the universe as a fragmented structure. This view has led all of us to be drawn to what I refer to as the "quantum of symptom disorders." Simply put, we focus on the superficial, outward experience of life to the exclusion of internal, metaphysical forces and energies.

Fortunately, the information revolution brought about by the Age of Aquarius is working in our favor. A growing proportion of the world's inhabitants are no longer accepting the mechanistic view of life. This is especially evident in the medical arena. Palliative treatments, which control symptoms of disorders without curing them, are no longer enough. Associating a particular illness with a specific part of the body draws attention away from the patient as a whole person. In the same manner, ascribing a societal problem to a particular person or group distracts us from our shared responsibility. Going even further, we must always look beyond our earth-bound environment to the effects of cosmic influence.

"THE ROOT OF ALL EVIL"

Our body consciousness is a channel for the Desire to Receive for Oneself Alone. Although the body is a physical entity, there is something lying beyond the mechanical operation of cells and molecules that causes it grow and function. This energy, as the Desire to Receive for Oneself Alone, is the "root of all evil" in the sense that it is this force and this consciousness that impose on us the limitations of time, space, and motion. Like the force of gravity, this energy seeks to swallow everything in its reach. The tools with which we can render ourselves invulnerable to this assault are therefore critical to our physical and mental well-being.

Kabbalah teaches that vulnerability is the opening that is directly responsible for inviting and manifesting a negative cosmic attack. Let us take cancer as an example. Everyone produces abnormal cells in the body from time to time. This can be attributed either to external factors or to a distortion of cellular functioning. Normally, the body's immune system keeps close watch for any abnormal cells and destroys them. For cancer to manifest as a disease, the immune system must therefore be inhibited in some way. The important point is this: Something is happening in a person who contracts cancer that creates vulnerability.

Factors such as stress, diet, and environment may play a role in the incidence of this disease. But none of these factors fully explains why particular individuals, at particular points in their lives, attract the production of cancerous cells, or why their body's defenses fail to eliminate them. There is no question about the strong links between the external factors mentioned above and cancer. But not everyone who experiences stress, poor diet, and other environmental influences gets cancer—and in fact, most do not. In our study of Kabbalah, we must therefore recognize the primacy of other factors. We must answer questions that real patients ask, such as "Why me?" and "Why now?" Why does one patient die while another recovers? Indeed, the questions often raised concerning disease are essentially the same ones we might introduce with regard to airplane accidents or any other apparently random misfortune.

When vulnerability in the form of an inner empty space expresses itself in an individual human being, it is exactly what the negative side has been waiting for. Very often the attack that results takes the form of physical illness, with the inner void manifesting itself as a lapse in the body's defenses. Negative energy disables the body's immune system. This is the determining factor governing why one person incurs a disease and another does not.

THE FIVE SENSES: A KABBALISTIC VIEW

Earth's atmosphere is continually bombarded by cosmic rays and cascades of energy from outer space, destroying and creating in a rhythmic choreography of energy. The future of humanity rests on the way the sky treats us—and in fact the celestial influence is already a part of our everyday consciousness. It is common knowledge, for example, that the sun and the moon exert a profound influence on our lives. The moon causes the sea to rise and fall with the tides. Sunspots and solar flares can affect earthly communication systems. For the kabbalist, these and all other energy-intelligences are always interrelated and bound up with each other. In our world they appear in different manifestations, but they are essentially parts of a unified whole. Our tendency to separate the physical and metaphysical worlds is seen by the kabbalist as a fundamental illusion.

In the kabbalistic view, our five senses are intrinsically dynamic in nature. The kabbalist sees these functions as acting outside ourselves in addition to providing us with the opportunity to experience the world around us. Our five senses are energy-intelligences that affect our environment just as they, in turn, are affected by it.

It is not surprising that the Ari, Rav Isaac Luria, constructed an intellectual map of sensory reality in which four of the five major senses are referred to as "basic." They are sight, hearing, smell, and speech, and they are enlivened by the four energy-intelligences of the Light. These energy-intelligences are known by their code names: Soul of Soul (sight), Soul (hearing), Spirit (smell) and Crude Spirit (speech).

The eyes, states the Ari, portray the most significant aspect and intensity of the Light. Consequently, the energy-intelligence generated by the eye can easily be transmitted to another person or thing. If, for example, the energy to be transferred is of a negative nature, and if the individual receiving this transmission has no security shield set up or at that moment has a breach in the immune system, he or she is vulnerable to attack. At that very moment, whatever is flying through the atmosphere becomes a threat.

THE POWER OF THE EYE: FOR EVIL AND FOR GOOD

The Evil Eye is very similar to a heat-seeking missile that locks onto an enemy plane and then destroys it. Once the deadly negative energy takes root in an individual, immense damage can take place.

Fortunately, the power of the eye can be just as effective as a healing instrument. Laser technology, which is replacing many conventional surgical procedures, is an expression of this power.

Lasers can reach the bones and internal organs without the need for an incision. From a kabbalistic perspective, of course, both the positive and negative potential of visual energy is nothing new. The Bible and *The Zohar* are replete with discussions of the awesome power of observation and the Evil Eye.

But how and why does energy transmission by the Evil Eye create such misfortune? Where does the force of the Evil Eye originate? *The Zohar* describes the Evil Eye as the ability of one person to attack another by projecting negative energy-intelligence. If someone you know thinks negatively of you, this eye channeling can affect both your physical and mental well-being. The energy-intelligence of a negative eye can stretch far and wide, creating turmoil in the form of "accidents" or other events.

The Evil Eye can also come into play without any negative intention. There are people who may not wish you harm, but because of a particular emptiness or void in themselves, they project this wanting as a negative energy. For example, a childless woman may mentally focus her own pain on the children of others. In fact, it is children who are most vulnerable to negative energy-intelligence. Kabbalah teaches that the reason for this vulnerability in children is rooted in the absence of the Desire to Share, which does not become an integral part of the soul until age 13 for boys and age 12 for girls.

Until that time, the Desire to Receive for Oneself Alone has dominion over the consciousness of children. Children indiscriminately draw all forms of energy to themselves, since they are inherently "takers." At maturity, when the Desire to Receive for the Purpose of Sharing also becomes an element in the psyche, the mental structure of a young person becomes balanced until such time as negative activity enters into their personalities. However, this form of vulnerability based on the Desire to Receive is not limited to children. We must always be aware of danger zones, caused by our negative activity makes us vulnerable. And we must be especially careful during periods of intensely negative planetary influences.

BEYOND THE MIND-BODY SPLIT

We must now move beyond the Cartesian separation between mind and body, between what is "within" and what is "outside." Yes, the Cartesian method has wrought many spectacular successes for our material well being—but any individual afflicted with heart disease or cancer would be more than willing to forsake material luxuries in exchange for a better understanding of health and illness. This idea is clearly stated in *The Zohar*:

> When there is separation of thought between the internal (*Zeir Anpin*) level of existence and its external (*Malkhut*), trouble and great pain reign in the world. When there is no separation, perfection, peace and harmony are dominant.

Our experience of life is determined less by physical reality than by the unrecognized influences of our own unconscious mind. In the traditional Cartesian view, it is assumed that this apparatus is basically the same for all of us. This was and remains a basic error—for there are individuals who can instantly sense and distinguish the vibrations of an environment while others simply feel nothing. The vibrations that some of us intuitively sense are the energy-intelligence underlying people or physical settings.

We must come to the realization that there are essentially two realities. The material, external reality lends itself to a reductionist perspective—the Cartesian view that everything is like a machine constructed from separate parts. The other reality—the 99 percent internal reality—has not been deemed worthy of scientific investigation. This other reality is what many scientists, with the important exception of the most advanced scientific thinkers, find so difficult to embrace.

But since the reductionist and materialist approach is inadequate to the task of solving the most serious problems facing humanity, how can the situation change? Transcending the limited view of our universe will require a major cultural revolution. Fortunately, that revolution is now under way in this Age of Aquarius, as recognized and forecast by Rav Shimon Bar Yohai, the author of *The Zohar*. The paradigm formulated in *The Zohar* by Rav Shimon has the potential to spiritually and materially unite all humanity. To develop a kabbalistic approach for the improvement of our individual and collective well-being, we need not break completely new ground. Rather, we can integrate Zoharic knowledge with the basic laws and principles established within the scientific community.

This new paradigm in scientific thought will lead to a truly kabbalistic view of reality in which knowledge of the human mind and body—and understanding of the unseen planetary influences—become integral parts of our lifestyles. In addition, we must achieve an awareness that our entire universe is in a natural state of dynamic balance. In maintaining this balance, the human species is the decisive factor. The Power of You is what really makes the movie.

Kabbalah teaches that before the wheel, there was the idea of the wheel. Not only do thoughts and ideas enable us to create physicality, but those same thoughts influence everything that occurs in the cosmos. We know that the moon affects the tides. We acknowledge that supernovas, black holes, and other phenomena in outer space inevitably affect weather and other conditions here on earth. But can humanity comprehend the kabbalistic principle that the behavior of people can override extraterrestrial influences and even sway intergalactic events? For the first time in many centuries, I believe that humanity can indeed grasp this essential truth. The destruction by the Romans of the Second Temple in Jerusalem in the year 70 of the Common Era was the cause of intellectual and spiritual darkness. Through the centuries that followed, the Light of Kabbalah flickered, but it could never be extinguished. *The Zohar* tells us that Kabbalah would have to await the coming of the Age of Aquarius before it could reappear as a powerful tool in the hands of humanity. Now that time has come. Now, as it is written,

> . . . *the eyes of the blind shall be opened,*
> *and the ears of the deaf shall hear.*
> *Then shall the lame man leap like a deer.*
> *And the tongue of the dumb shall sing.*
> —Isaiah 35:5-6

"THE BITTER CONDITIONS OF HEALING . . ."

Beyond the slightest doubt, the promise from the Book of Isaiah with which we closed the previous chapter will be fulfilled. This assurance was clearly made by the Ari in his *Gates of the Holy Spirit*:

> To remove an illness, one must take upon oneself the bitter conditions of healing, for the purpose of grasping the metaphysical teachings which are the secret doctrines of the world. This is the wisdom that has been concealed from the days of Rav Shimon Bar Yohai until now [1572], and as the Rashbi (Rav Shimon Bar Yohai) stated, "Permission shall not be granted concerning its revelation until the final generation that will usher in the Age of Aquarius [which time is now], through the medium of the Teacher Rav Isaac Luria, with the assistance of the prophetic spirit within him."

The human nervous system is a supremely complex structure. An almost infinite number of interconnections and electrical impulses permit us to think, act, create, and, most important, understand who we really are. An enormous volume of research has been directed toward understanding the connection between mental activity and our physical body.

This research indicates that the mind actively participates in curing sickness and maintaining health. Psychic imbalance is seen as the root of all illness. Consequently, stress has come to be seen as the fundamental and primary issue underlying mental or physical well-being. However, we have already addressed this phenomenon and have concluded that stress is not the primary cause of the ills that befall us in our present environment. If it were the primary cause, why are some people stressed and others are not when all are in the same environmental setting?

Today, a small but strong minority of scientists understand illness in terms of a mind-body connection. Yet Kabbalah always takes this understanding even one step further, to the "power of mind over matter." The kabbalists tell us that humanity can determine the nature of both physical and metaphysical reality. Yet the vast resources of modern medicine lead us to doubt whether we can have a significant impact on our own well-being. Although the achievements of modern medical science should by no means be downplayed, holistic techniques that include the mind, heart, and cosmos will, in the future, play an ever-increasing role in advancing human well-being.

The kabbalistic principle of mind over matter is not necessarily congruent with the popular meaning of this phrase. Telekinesis, for example, is a methodology that affects physical objects through the power of thought alone. Although the bending of a spoon is certainly within the realm of practical possibility, Kabbalah holds that it is not a worthy pursuit. A far more productive use of thought-energy is that which allows us to become engaged with an infinite reality—for by doing so, we can take control of our own destiny and that of the whole cosmos.

Activating the power of mind over matter requires that we undergo a basic alteration of consciousness. This entails a transformation of the mind from the rational, logical mode, which involves five to seven percent of our potential, to the cosmic mode, which allows us to transcend physical limitations and restraints. The energy of thought can traverse great distances; it can affect people and objects and is indeed a tangible factor in the world around us. Through this same power, we can also remove ourselves from the negative influences of degenerative disease. Since Kabbalah establishes the cause of all illness in the negative energy-intelligence of the cosmos, the task of the kabbalist is to rise above these negative influences. Moreover, the fulfillment of that task lies within our grasp. The stars certainly impel us, but they do not compel us.

THE KREBIOZEN "CURE"

Kabbalah places great emphasis on the awesome power of thought to the extent that even objects and experiences are also subject to thought's energy-intelligence. Mind and body, thought and environment are inseparable. When a person falls ill, it is therefore not just the disease that must be treated, but the entire self.

One of the most dramatic cases illustrating the power of mind over body was reported more than half a century ago by Dr Bruno Klopfer, a researcher involved in the testing of a drug known as Krebiozen. In 1950, Krebiozen had received sensational national publicity as a "cure" for cancer; it was being tested by the American Medical Association and by the United States Food and Drug Administration. One of Dr. Klopfer's patients had developed advanced lymphatic cancer, with tumor masses throughout his body. When the patient learned that Dr. Klopfer was involved with Krebiozen, he begged to be given the drug. After just one dose, his tumors disappeared. His recovery was astonishing, and he regained enough strength to resume a normal life.

When published reports of the AMA and FDA claimed that the drug was ineffective, however, the patient took a dramatic turn for the worse. His cancer returned, and he once again became bedridden. In a desperate attempt to save him, his physician told him that the reports were false and that double-strength doses of Krebiozen would produce better results. Actually, the injections consisted of sterile water. But the patient again experienced rapid remission, and once again the tumor masses melted. Soon he even went back to his hobby of flying.

Then the FDA announced its final findings, which appeared in the media as follows: "Tests conclusively show Krebiozen is worthless in the treatment of cancer." The man died a few days later.

How can this "placebo effect" be explained? Science is only now beginning to map the routes between the brain and other parts of the body. But there can be no doubt that the mind acts as a healer as well as a destroyer. Taking this idea one step further, Kabbalah suggests that the mind can extend its influence over the entire cosmos. *The Zohar* clearly states that the cosmic influences that lie at the heart of all misfortune and illness should be subject to human control. These influences can be made to behave in accordance with humanity's directives. Kabbalistic teachings demonstrate how people can exercise substantial influence over medical conditions that were once considered to lie beyond conscious control.

UNSEEN INFLUENCES, REAL DANGERS

To truly understand illness, we must consider not only what causes disease, but also why most people are able to avoid it in the first place. We are all vulnerable to all sorts of diseases. This does not, however, mean that we will become sick. The body's defense system is so powerful and effective that most people exposed to all sorts of infectious agents maintain their health. This is the dilemma facing medical research: In one case the body does battle with foreign substances and subsequently destroys them. In another, with the same self-healing system, the body's defense mechanism fails to fight. Vulnerability is the kabbalist's explanation. The cosmos, at definite times, attacks and suppresses our natural defense mechanisms. The body's immune system, which keeps close tabs on abnormal cells and then homes in for the kill, can be inhibited by negative cosmic influences. The important point here is that an unseen influence creates susceptibility.

So what is to be done? Over the centuries, kabbalists have developed highly refined diagnostic tools for our physical selves, as well as a unique art of kabbalistic Meditation that allows for the connection of mental activity with the physical body and the universe. This is hugely important, for it is highly unlikely that the mysteries of thought and consciousness will ever be unraveled by conventional scientific methods. Although contemporary science has discarded the duality of body and mind, the investigation of the brain has left it in awe of the mind.

ONCE AGAIN: "AS ABOVE, SO BELOW"

If we track the cycles of terrestrial life and identify those cycles, the curious fluctuations that emerge suggest a metaphysical pattern closely resembling that of the DNA in our physical bodies. In other words, the planets and signs of the zodiac make their celestial imprint on the face of earth. The knowable, observable shell of each planet is, according to *The Zohar*, an aspect of body consciousness. As a result, the limitations pertaining to the body consciousness of man also apply to the celestial realm. Body consciousness, whether it exists in the human realm or in the celestial, causes the buildup of layer upon layer of negativity. The greater the Desire to Receive for Oneself Alone, the blinder we become to the Light.

The illusion of darkness brought on by body consciousness is the cause of our problems and difficulties. Placed in a position or condition of vulnerability, humanity robotically gives in to the body consciousness of celestial influence. When negative influences of the celestial region reign over the universe, humanity, without the benefit of a security shield, becomes inundated with chaos, disorder, and misfortune. Even physical health may be placed in jeopardy. If, for example, the Desire to Receive for Oneself Alone overtakes a person during the zodiacal domination of Cancer, that individual has connected with the energy of cancer. Thus, from a kabbalistic standpoint, the dreaded disease had its origin during the reign of the zodiac sign of Cancer.

It is no accident that Abraham the Patriarch designated the fourth sign of the Zodiac with the name of Cancer. Furthermore, Cancer's sign of the crab, which manifests during the Hebrew month of *Tammuz*, holds deep significance. The purpose of the crab's appearance in the heavenly constellations is to lend insight into this month's body consciousness.

A good starting point for our investigation into the body consciousness of the crab is its mode of locomotion. In walking or crawling, most members of the crab group display the peculiar characteristic of a sidelong gait—an unusual way of getting from one place to another! Looking more closely at this, we see that there are some marked differences between walking forward and walking sideways. The distance covered is far greater in forward motion. When one is walking sideways, only one foot or side can be in motion at the same time, and continuous activity does not occur in a sidelong journey.

What does this distinctive characteristic imply? Crawling sideways prevents continuous motion as opposed to forward movement. Before the left side commences its activity, the right side must come to a complete halt. Try walking sideways in a leftward direction. Before you can set your left foot in motion, your right foot must rest alongside the left foot, and for a moment your body must come to a complete standstill. When you walk in a forward position, however, both feet are always moving. Soul consciousness exists as a continuous circuitry of energy,

without any interruption in its flow. Body consciousness represents and symbolizes a constant illusion of an interrupted, fragmented flow of energy-intelligence that results in chaos and disorder. Domination by the Desire to Receive for Oneself Alone
is the nature of the crab. And the crab's internal essence of body
consciousness is physically manifested in its form of movement.

The essential problem of cancer as an illness arises when the
energy-intelligence of a Desire to Receive for Oneself Alone
invades the unity of an individual. The cells of a human body
were created as, and connected with, an all-embracing, unified
whole of soul consciousness. During the course of a lifetime, if
an individual becomes vulnerable to the short circuitry of the
Desire to Receive for Oneself Alone during the month of
Cancer, he or she falls victim to the disease of cancer. The loss
of a loved one or other misfortunes thrust the individual into a
state of depression. A lack of fulfillment overcomes the person.
This condition creates an affinity dominated entirely by body
consciousness. When one is totally consumed by matters of the
flesh, the illness is given permission to enter.

The point that I am making is that celestial influence combines
a dual form of energy-intelligence. The positive or soul consciousness of celestial entities regulates and determines the
brighter, happier moments of our existence. Body consciousness, on the other hand, represents the darker side of existence,
invoking and exerting the influence of chaos, disease, and misfortune in our lives. At this point, the individual may seek an
illusory, temporary means of alleviating the pressures brought on
by causes that seem unknowable. In reality, of course, the culprit

and underlying cause lie within the body consciousness of the celestial region, not within the terrestrial plane.

If a solution to a problem does not include an accurate description or understanding of the metaphysical origin of that problem, it is not a viable solution. Symptomatic reasoning simply ignores the true causes of the seeming enigmas that confront humanity.

But there is an even more serious problem with the biomedical approach. Virtually every medication available includes a warning with regard to its potential side effects. In point of fact, the body often vigorously resists medications. Chemotherapy can provoke resistance in cancer cells, making them more malignant. Over time, antibiotics can actually strengthen bacteria. Although I do not mean to imply that all drug therapy is wrong, I am suggesting what *The Zohar* implies: The origins of degeneration can be traced to the internal energy-intelligence of body consciousness, which is the Desire to Receive for Oneself Alone. Acute and traumatic conditions of a life-threatening nature should be attributed to this energy-intelligence. And these conditions can be corrected by connecting with the positive energy-intelligence of our soul consciousness, which is the Desire to Receive for the Purpose of Sharing.

THE IMMUNITY TIMELINE

The startling revelations of *The Zohar* provide answers to all the mysteries of creation, including the anatomy of man. With *The Zohar* as our guide, for example, we can understand why everyone is born with an intact but underdeveloped immune system that matures shortly after birth. After leaving the haven of the mother's womb—where it was protected by watery fluid and fed by the mother—the newborn infant is left vulnerable to attack by the *Yetzer Ha'ra*, the negative energy-intelligence. This negative energy-intelligence immediately attaches itself to the child, which now lacks the protection previously conferred by the mother. Once we understand this, we grasp the vital role of the thymus gland: to provide the security shield necessary to protect the infant's immune system.

Upon reaching the age of puberty, however, the *Yetzer Ha'Tov*, or positive energy-intelligence, now dwells within the child and provides the necessary security shield. Consequently, there is no longer a need for the thymus gland. It is at this point that the soul consciousness of the individual is brought into the scenario. Health will now depend on whether a person's consciousness and actions are of a positive or a negative nature.

One of the mysteries of the immune system is a peculiar phenomenon linked to the vital role of the thymus gland. The thymus—which actually consists of two oval-shaped lobes—appears in early infancy behind the infant's breastbone. The thymus is responsible for the development of the immune system. During the gestational period, the immune system of the fetus is supplemented by factors acquired from the mother's milk, whose internal energy-intelligence is dominated by positive essence.

After birth, the thymus gland produces cells called lymphocytes that recognize and protect the body's own tissues while at the same time initiating an immune response to disease. Strangely, at puberty—or at approximately 13 years of age for boys and 12 years of age for girls—the role of producing these lymphocytes shifts to the lymph nodes, spleen, and bone marrow. Why does this occur, and why at this age? Insight into this strange phenomenon, especially in light of the growing interest in the importance of the immune system, may be found in *The Zohar*. There we learn that at the moment a child is born into the world, the *Yetzer Ha'ra* (the embodiment of negative energy-intelligence) attaches itself to the child to drain away the Light; as it is written, "sin croucheth at the door." Here "at the door" refers to the opening of the uterus that accompanies the birth of the child. The term "sin" is a code name for the negative energy-intelligence, which was also referred to as sin by King David in the verse "And my sin is ever before me."

Positive energy-intelligence first comes to us only when we begin to purify ourselves. What day is that? When a boy reaches his 13th birthday or when a girl reaches her 12th. From that time on, we find ourselves attended by two companions: one on the right and the other on the left; one positive and the other negative. These two angels are appointed to keep us company continually. When a person makes a choice to do good, the evil inducer bows to him. The right gains dominion over the left, and the two angels join hands to offer protection in all ways. As it is written, "For He will give his angels charge over you, to keep you in all your ways."

Scripture states, "Better is a poor and wise child than an old and foolish king, who knoweth not how to receive warning." The "child" here signifies the positive intelligence, who is so called because he is, as it were, a youngster by the side of man, whom he does not join until the age of 13 years. "He is better than an old and foolish king" refers to the evil intelligence, which is called "king and ruler over the sons of men." As soon as people are born and see the light of day, the evil attaches itself to them. For this reason, the evil intelligence is referred to as "old." And people are called "foolish" for not knowing how to receive warning. As King Solomon wrote, "The fool walketh in darkness."

THE DIFFERENCE BETWEEN SICKNESS AND HEALTH

Much has been written in recent years about the human immune system, and about why some of us are more vulnerable than others to its breakdown. Here again, the workings of "bad luck" remain mysterious when we explore the reasons some and not others become exposed to its fury. Victims of drug and alcohol addiction are often described as weak-minded people who fall prey to influences over which they have no control. Yet Kabbalistically speaking, people who succumb to drugs are really looking for a free adventure into spirituality without the use of Restriction. Hence, as the need for more and more stimulation takes hold, real needs are less and less fulfilled.

Physicians and psychologists want to explain states of illness or addiction as they appear without exploring the question of why some people are affected and others not. It is unfortunate that these experts do not examine the role of cosmic influence and reincarnation. If we do nothing more than chart these patients' activities in daily life, together with negative cosmic danger zones, we will find some exciting differences between the way the so-called lucky ones become and remain immune while the so-called unlucky ones are rendered vulnerable.

There are three special differences to be investigated: first, the lunar-solar months in which people are born; second, when and if negative behavior and activity took place during these cosmic danger zones; and third and most important, the security shield against attack from negative energy-intelligence. Before examining the mystery of these phenomena, let us first explore the kabbalistic viewpoint regarding the idea of a metaphysical security shield, the likes of which would seem to exist only in science-fiction novels. A good starting point for our investigation is, as always, *The Zohar* itself:

> When Jacob departed from Laban, all the holy legions surrounded him so that he was not left by himself. Rav Hizkiah asked: If that was so, why was Jacob, as stated later, "left alone"? Said Rav Yehudah in reply: Because he exposed himself deliberately to danger, and therefore the guardian angels [the security shield] deserted him. It was to this that he (Jacob) alluded when he said: I am not worthy of all the mercies and of all the truth which thou hast shown thy servant. Rav Elazar said: The sages have stated that on that night and at that hour the power of Esau [negative energy-intelligence] was ascendant, and therefore Jacob was left alone [meaning vulnerable]!

Assuming that we become familiar with those negative points of time, how do we avoid falling into the trap that has been laid for us? Let us turn again to the Zoharic text, which can and does provide all of humankind with the necessary tools to deal with those unseen negative energy-intelligence forces:

> Rav Shimon opened a discourse on the verse: Better is he that is lightly esteemed, and has a servant, than he that plays the man of rank, and lacketh bread. This verse, he said, speaks of the Dark Lord, the evil prompter, who lays plots and unceasingly brings up accusations against man. He puffs up a man's heart, encouraging him to arrogance and conceit, to carry his head high, until the negative side obtains dominion over him. Better, therefore, is one who is "lightly esteemed" and remains humble in heart and spirit. The evil prompter is bowed down before such a man, and so far is the Dark Lord from obtaining mastery over the man that it is man who obtains mastery over him. As it is written: "But thou mayest rule over him."

"He who is lightly esteemed" is exemplified by Jacob, who humbled himself before Esau so that Esau should in time become his servant. If we are to become masters of our destinies, then let us learn the cardinal rule: Effort is required on our part! We have become a society that seeks to obtain instant relief simply by paying for it. This approach leads us toward disaster. There are no shortcuts or easy methods for achieving permanency in our well-being. To avoid the work and the responsibilities that come with this mastery, we are drawn to measures that provide only temporary relief.

All spiritual techniques, including the tools of Kabbalah, serve as a secondary application toward improving our physical and mental well-being. The primary and initial step that must be taken lies in a resolve to develop a positive attitude toward our fellow man and environment. With the cosmos filled with negative energy-intelligence created by man's negative activity, we find it very difficult to resist and operate against the stream of negative energy. Kabbalistic meditative techniques will go a long way toward providing assistance in overcoming these obstacles. But mastery requires knowledge and resolve. In order for us to change the quality of our lives, we must first change the nature of our behavior.

CHAPTER SIX:

STRESS

PSYCHIC PAIN

Psychic pain is one of the dominant realities of our lives today. By this I mean all the misery, depression, and malaise that for the sake of convenience we call stress. The prevalence of stress is evidenced by the enormous interest on the part of the health care industry in providing drugs for it, and of the entertainment industry in offering distractions from it.

For all its action and excitement, and despite its great accomplishments, our modern lifestyle generates conditions that corrode the body and the spirit. Pressures of all kinds take their toll, taxing the body's essential resources and draining its energy— and that's just the physical level. Stress also brings about a process of inner deterioration that saps the very foundation of our emotional and spiritual selves. Marriages begin to suffer, "nervous breakdowns" take place, careers are ruined. In a turbulent search for stimulation, more and more people fall prey to anxiety, mental illness, or drug and alcohol abuse.

Despite all the material comfort that has been achieved through technological advances, technology has failed to enable us to attain the fulfillment we desire and need. This strain on millions of individuals translates into a huge weight that bears down on society at large. The annual financial cost of this burden has been estimated to be as high as $150 billion. The human cost cannot be calculated.

Yet Kabbalah teaches that we have the power to change things for the better. We can accomplish this simply by changing ourselves. This change takes place at every level of being—physical, emotional, and spiritual. It transcends the mechanistic perspective on life, in which illness and stress are treated as breakdowns in a mechanical system. The human body possesses an inherent healing ability; good health is its natural state. But this is a message that the medical profession has been unwilling to hear. The notion that we are self-healers is not promoted. Instead, we are encouraged to depend on a health care system that is already overburdened and is certain to become even more so. This applies to psychiatry and psychotherapy as well as to surgery and every other medical discipline.

Ironically, because of their mechanistic and fragmented view of health, physicians themselves often suffer more intensely in their personal lives than anyone else. From the very start, their medical education and training generate a high degree of stress, yet they are taught nothing about how to cope with it.

Most of our society's mental and physical problems have a stress-related component. Yet nowhere is there more confusion, misinformation, and lack of direction concerning both the causes of stress and its treatment than in the worlds of psychiatry and medicine. For example, our high incidence of heart disease illustrates the disappointing results that medicine has achieved in dealing with stress-related diseases.

Stress is responsible for the breakdown of the natural biorhythm upon which health depends. There are even researchers who view every illness as originating from stress-related problems. Yet researchers are currently at a loss to identify the causes of stress, or even to define what it really is. As a rule, when people attempt to describe the pressures of stress, what they are really talking about is some situation in their lives that has placed them under a great deal of tension. financial difficulties, family problems, job insecurity, and a host of other things can cause stress. But researchers have had little or no success in establishing what stress itself really is.

The experts' definitions do little more than describe our reaction to the situations that are responsible for creating stress within us. Trying to define stress is obviously quite different from defining something in the material realm. For physical objects, we can provide a description of specific properties or characteristics. Stress, however, remains very much in the realm of metaphysics. Since the German physicist Werner Heisenberg shocked the scientific world many years ago with his well-known uncertainty principle, the fact that we cannot "know everything" has engendered considerable anxiety for most of us. What worries one person might not worry another, but there's no doubt that everyone today has something to feel anxious about. Some people worry when crossing the street. Others refuse to leave their homes for fear of what might happen outside. Each of us is concerned with what the future holds. Uncertainty permeates our thoughts and feelings.

The extension of the biomedical approach in physical medicine to the treatment of mental illness has been equally unsuccessful. Attempts to arrive at a basic diagnostic system for mental disorders have in large part been wasteful, for physically based diagnoses will prove futile for most mental disorders. Standard psychiatric practice interferes with the healing process by suppressing the symptoms. True therapy should consist of facilitating the body's natural healing process by providing a supportive atmosphere for the patient from both an emotional and a metaphysical perspective. Rather than suppress the process that comprises symptoms, the symptoms should be allowed to intensify in order to allow for a proper evaluation and prognosis.

The Cartesian perspective of medical researchers often prevents them from observing the beneficial aspects and potential value of illness. This narrow view fails to take into account the subtle spiritual and psychological aspects of mental disorders, thereby preventing researchers from arriving at methods for truly healing the mentally ill.

"PHYSICIAN, HEAL THYSELF"

It is both intriguing and ironic that physicians themselves suffer the most as a result of this Cartesian view of health and disease. Often they completely disregard the stressful circumstances in their own lives. Physicians have high rates not only of physical illness, but also of alcoholism, suicide, and other social pathologies.

The problem of stress for doctors, and for society as a whole, is a direct result of our evasion of the essential issue: "What is stress, and why does it affect some and not others?" The failure to ask "why" at the deepest level is the fundamental cause of this immense societal problem. From a kabbalistic standpoint, an understanding of stress cannot originate from within the body's physiological mechanisms.

Most clinical researchers believe that when people are subjected to stress, the body responds by activating defense mechanisms such as heart rate and blood pressure increases in efforts to help the body defend itself. But if we go to the movies and see a horror film, our heart begins to beat faster, our breathing becomes irregular, and our blood pressure climbs. Is the movie the stress factor, or does stress consist of the changes our physical bodies undergo? Although medical professionals can identify the biochemical variations that occur during some external stress reactions, they cannot explain how stress activates the nervous system. Nor can they explain why our nerves act on some parts of our body and not on others. Furthermore, why are some people affected by such films while others are not?

Physicians are concerned with the treatment of the body. Psychiatrists and psychologists are concerned with the healing of the mind. The Cartesian gap between the two hampers our understanding of the role stress plays in the development of both physical and mental illness. The connection between mental states and cancer, for example, has been known for centuries. The reason for the lack of communication between physical health professionals and psychiatrists essentially lies in the lack of confidence physicians have in dealing with patients on a metaphysical or even an emotional level. The truth is, many physicians look down on psychiatrists and consider them second-rate doctors. Mental activity is seen as a secondary phenomenon—if it is considered at all.

It is little wonder, then, that the stress factor in medicine remains a misunderstood phenomenon. Stress, which is basically a metaphysical experience, is neglected altogether by the Cartesian science of medicine.

The so-called psychological stress that arises from unhappy relationships is, from a kabbalistic view, nothing more than a symptom of a deeper problem. Stress that seems to originate from problematic human interactions, such as conflicts with a boss or a mother-in-law, do not universally arise from the seemingly obvious source. For example, a mother-in-law is not an inherently stressful relative. One can, on occasion, have a pleasant relationship with a mother-in-law.

During the Age of Aquarius, *The Zohar* offers greater hope than a scientific establishment that, under the influence of Heisenberg, accepts universal randomness and improbability. *The Zohar* provides a direct link to the universal energy-intelligence that is the Creator's Light. In fact, what lies in store is an overload of energy-intelligence much more intense than anything experienced in the past.

IRRESISTIBLE POISON

The problems of addiction and substance abuse affect the entire socioeconomic spectrum. Doctors, lawyers, athletes, corporate executives, students, housewives—it would seem that no one is immune to this menace. Staggering numbers of people from all walks of life are addicted to prescription drugs, diet pills, and sleep medications. Millions more smoke marijuana or take cocaine on a daily basis. Alcoholism continues to be an international plague. Hundreds of thousands of people die each year in the United States from diseases related to tobacco addiction. Yet no one is even considering, much less addressing, the true cause of this addiction epidemic.

Clearly, stress is a key factor influencing the formation of addictive behaviors. But in a given environment, why are some people "stressed out" while others are not? Must we explain this away with the truism that one person is "lucky" in his or her genetic makeup while another person is not? Obviously, this deterministic reasoning leaves little room for free will.

It is useful to note that indigenous cultures have always developed methods of transcendence—songs, dances, and other rituals—in order to reduce societal stress. These cultures have been capable of creating security shields that can protect them from stress. But in our own culture, what was once a rich social and spiritual fabric has been eaten away by empty material concepts and false technological promises, ultimately to be eradicated altogether by the great myth called "progress." Today, our once-intimate relationship with nature has been supplanted by a cornucopia of so-called recreational drugs and electronic distractions.

Kabbalists have long known that our thoughts shape what we perceive as reality every bit as much as reality shapes our thoughts. We are more than mere observers of reality, and we are much more than mere spectators of our earthly conception of what is real. Our observations and actions, according to kabbalistic wisdom, not only determine the earthly reality we choose to create but also mold the way in which we choose to interact with that reality. It is we who produce and direct our own movie—the same movie in which we ourselves are the stars.

CREATING THE VESSEL

By reading or scanning *The Zohar*, we can re-create ourselves as a Vessel that is fully capable of receiving this awesome power without being burned out in the process. But a question that might now be going through your mind is, "How can I possibly use *The Zohar*? I can't even read the Hebrew letters. I don't have the slightest idea what the words mean!"

Actually, it's easy to deal with these concerns. Take a trip down to the supermarket and observe the scanner at the checkout counter. As the cashier will tell you, the scanner relays information detected on the product bar code to a computer that transmits the purchase price back to the cash register—almost at the speed of light. This is precisely the relationship that exists between what we see when we scan *The Zohar* and what is received by the "computers" of our minds. Scanning *The Zohar* immediately establishes the information in our mental software. What's more, we now possess the software program through which we can connect to a reality in which the constraints of time, space, and entropy are erased once and for all—and where chaos and uncertainty simply do not exist.

The kabbalist sees the struggle of science to achieve a "theory of everything" as a reflection of man's striving to shed the garments of darkness and step once again into the Light. Science, from a kabbalistic perspective, expresses an inborn human tendency to strip away the stifling raiment of physicality and to embrace the Infinite. Out attraction to the Light never ceases. It is forever drawing us toward the culmination of the cosmic process, the final *Tikkune*. In this Age of Aquarius, the energy of the Light intensifies with each passing day. And the greater the Light's revelation, the greater the pressure on us to reveal it.

This increase in pressure signals the beginning of the end of a long, arduous process of spiritual adjustment and rectification and, for many individuals, the dawning of a New Age. Consequently, the fundamental cause of stress is the presence of a huge opportunity for fulfillment. In this Age of Aquarius, the Light no longer curtails its Desire to Share, nor does It consider the present limits of our capacity to receive fulfillment. The Light now directs its full and complete potential for fulfillment toward us. This is an unmatched opportunity—but there is also the possibility of severe burnout for those who are unprepared.

Thus, *The Zohar* declares the paradoxical circumstances that surround humanity during the Age of Aquarius: "Woe and blessing unto those who shall be present in that age." *The Zohar* explains that it will be a time of blessing for those people who have taken control of the Desire to Receive for Oneself Alone.

Stress is a manifestation of the Light struggling to fulfill humanity's most basic desire. The only way to end stress once and for all, therefore, is to gain that ultimate fulfillment. Medicine seeks only to relieve the symptoms of stress. This is attempted through the widespread use of tranquilizers and narcotics. If stress can fill a person's everyday activities with anxiety and dissatisfaction, the assumption is that the relief of stress will bring about tranquillity.

It has become all too obvious, however, that this has not been the case. We have been programmed from birth to look for fast (and temporary) relief. In so doing, however, we fall prey to an avalanche of unforeseen and sometimes overwhelming problems. We are constantly "on the run," preoccupied with fleeing stressful situations. Yet for most of us, the possibility of achieving a permanent solution seems as remote as ever. This book proposes that you can achieve that permanent solution by encouraging even greater stress. Increased stress is an indication that a greater degree of Light is destined for you. Yet the idea of seeking out stress seems contrary to our every instinct.

But consider this analogy. Suppose you have decided to open a manufacturing business that requires heavy machinery. If this is the case, you would need to be aware of the stress capabilities of the floor that supports the machines. Assuming that the machines exceed the strength of the floor, would you decide to remove the necessary equipment and replace it with lighter models? Only a very poor manager would come to that conclusion. It would make much more sense to reinforce the existing floor so that it could safely carry the weight—or carry even more weight, should that become necessary.

In this analogy, the machinery represents the Light, while the floor symbolizes the Desire to Receive for Oneself Alone. Restriction or resistance to the oncoming fulfillment by the

Light is the prerequisite to the expansion of our Vessels. And to the extent that we successfully receive the Light's sharing, beneficent energy-intelligence, the rewards are translated into mental and physical well-being.

THE SEARCH FOR SERENITY

It is always self-defeating to explore methods by which stress— that is, the presence of the Light—can be reduced or even removed. The Light is not influenced by our desire to withdraw from its energy-intelligence. Its fundamental desire is to share, and nothing we do can prevent it from achieving that objective.

We must understand the real nature of stress. For many people, the Light may be experienced as an invader—one that makes unwanted demands on them. And while we may think that it is in our best interests to rid ourselves of this burden, in so doing we face the inevitable consequence of a possibility for diminished fulfillment.

By living in a state of diminished fulfillment, we must also expect to be in a constant state of frustration. This is because our natural desire to receive is being ignored. If we have not properly expanded our Vessel's dimensions of receiving, the Light places too much pressure on us. On the other hand, rejecting the Light's beneficence fails to satisfy our natural desire to receive true fulfillment, which is the real purpose of our lives. The use of alcohol, narcotics, tranquilizers, or other stress-relieving drugs is only a temporary expedient. The problem here lies in the "return trip," because the effects of artificial methods remain for only a limited time. Under the influence of drugs or other intoxicants, one can achieve a brief period of disentanglement from the body's essentially limiting and self-serving energy. But this cannot last when it is induced by artificial means.

The soul's consciousness is one of Desire to Receive for the Purpose of Sharing. The body's function, however, is to instill the consciousness of Desire to Receive for Oneself Alone. Consequently, when the effects of the intoxicants fade, the soul again experiences the limits imposed upon it by the body. Body consciousness, by its very nature, cannot manifest the desire to expand the dimensions of its Vessel.

The Light wishes to enter and embrace our souls, but it cannot do so without our active participation. This is the essential kabbalistic precept of "no coercion in spirituality." The soul, whose intent is to become united with the Light, must first transform the body's consciousness from a Desire to Receive for Oneself Alone to desire for the purpose of sharing. This can be stressful in terms of what we experience in our everyday lives—but once the process is completed, the presence of the Light no longer constitutes an "overload factor." Indeed, when our Vessel has been reinforced and reprogrammed, the opposite of stress may be expected.

Always remember: The Light will never fade away. It is and always will be there for us. But we must make room for its entrance into our own consciousness and into that of humanity as a whole. Connection with the Light in the Age of Aquarius is no longer intended only for those who merit Its influence. All of earth's inhabitants are now subject to the Light's demand for revelation. Our only real choice is to increase our Vessel to its maximum capacity and to embrace all of the Light Force destined for us.

Using artificial means to reduce our desire to receive does not influence the behavior of the Light. The Light will still make a continuous effort toward our fulfillment. This is simply "for our own good." The tensions of modern life are all based on our inability to bring the Light into our consciousness. The widespread use of addicting and harmful medications for the relief of excessive stress and related illness must be considered a complication of—not a solution to—the problem of stress. We must develop the full capability of harnessing the Light in order to achieve and sustain fulfillment in these trying times.

Without a doubt, the study of Kabbalah and the use of kabbalistic tools and teachings, when practiced properly, can enhance our day-to-day lives in ways that are beyond imagining.

CHAPTER SEVEN:

TIME

THE CLOCK HAS STOPPED

Today, scientists agree that the conventional view of time—that is, that which clocks measure—is finished. It has gone the way of all outdated scientific principles. But new concepts of time are pointing us toward a higher and more authentic view of reality. These signs indicate a world above the physical one: a world of consciousness; a world referred to in Genesis as the Tree of Life.

Tree of Life consciousness is the realm of pure awareness. The world of illusion, fragmentation, space, and time have no place within Tree of Life consciousness. Once we experience the true reality of the Tree of Life, we have removed the illusion of time and space. We at once reach every part of the universe where past, future, and present are one with the Light. *The Zohar* clearly demonstrates this view in the following passage:

> And he took from the stones of the place, and put them under his head and lay down in that place. And the Creator said, "The land on which thou liest, to thee I will give it!" Said Rav Isaac, "This verse teaches us that the entire Land of Israel was condensed and shrunk to the size of Jacob's body."

Hence the reality that Jacob lay on "the entire land"—that is, the Land of Israel!

To understand this, we must recognize the two great revolutions that gave birth to the new physics: quantum theory and the theory of relativity. The first casualty resulting from these theories was the belief that time is universal and absolute. What Einstein demonstrated was that time is in fact elastic and can be stretched and shrunk by motion. The second casualty resulting from these theories was that space is elastic as well. Few people would ever dream of the possibility that what is one foot today might be two feet tomorrow or that the same one foot of today may be one-half foot tomorrow. Yet not only does the theory of relativity demand that distances have no absolute and fixed dimension, it also suggests experiments to verify these discrepancies.

We all take for granted that we and all material things must be somewhere, someplace. When physicists began to explore the concept of location in light of quantum physics, they were shocked to find that the very idea was meaningless.

In line with *The Zohar*'s declaration that space is indeed illusory, I recall trying an experiment with a group of 150 people. We were going to walk to a place some 45 minutes away. The road we were to take had very little traffic. I suggested that we all lower our eyes and visualize the road passing under our feet, rather than our feet trekking along over the road. Everyone immediately sensed a kind of "remaining in the same place" with the road moving under us. The walk no longer consciously felt like 45 minutes—and most of us experienced no sense of motion whatsoever.

The problem we all face in our lives is the ill-advised programming that has come ot be built into our worldview. All the concepts of conventional science have been firmly rooted in the "common sense" world of daily experience. Time was time as we experienced it, and space was an obstacle to overcome in getting anywhere we wanted to go. When the new age of physics began to enter public consciousness in the early 1950s, however, cozy notions of reality that had endured for centuries were blown away. Many unquestioned assumptions were shattered. Suddenly the world was revealed as a weird and uncertain place. Common sense became an unreliable guide. The old mechanistic and rational universe collapsed and was replaced by a metaphysical world of paradox and uncertainty.

When the bizarre workings of the quantum world replaced a mechanistic universe, space and time were cast into the realm of metaphysics. The problem now was, "How do we face up to a reality that seems to oppose our preconceived, rational notions of how we expect the world to act?" There was also a fundamental question for both physicists and laypeople: "How do we retrain our thinking after having been told for centuries that there is no reality other than the physical one to which we usually relate?"

THE ILLUSION OF AGING

Kabbalah teaches that the so-called aging process is yet another example of the realm of time-bound illusion in which we live. With this awareness, we come to a very practical question: "How can we actually become younger?" Or, stated another way, "How can we maintain the perfect state of our existence? How do we capture the developmental stages from infancy to adulthood without paying the observable price of aging?"

We have come so far in the pursuit of scientific understanding; yet with all our wonderful discoveries, we are no closer to controlling our destinies. What does the nature of the universe have to do with our everyday lifestyle? How will understanding the cosmos enhance our mental and physical well-being?

Kabbalah raises questions about everything, but it also zeros in on the ideas that explain everything—from before the Big Bang to humanity's power to control the universe and, consequently, to control his own destiny. It is for this reason that Kabbalah and *The Zohar* have commanded such respect for almost 2,000 years.

The awesome power of Kabbalah has led some people to be fearful of delving into its secrets. This fear, according to many kabbalists, was well founded until the middle of the 16th century. From that period on, which kabbalists consider to be the beginning of the Age of Aquarius, the limitations and prohibitions surrounding kabbalistic study were completely removed. In our society, however, it is still the practice of teachers and parents to shy away from most of the questions raised by *The Zohar*. Many find themselves uncomfortable with the issues raised by Kabbalah. They fear the responsibilities that may be thrust upon them when they discover that, indeed, there exists the possibility of attaining control in their lives.

The Zohar is the infusion of energy that is necessary to revive us from our deep and long slumber. Einstein once stated to an interviewer, "All I want to know are the Lord's thoughts on how

He created the world. The rest is only details." *The Zohar* reveals the thought behind everything. *The Zohar* brings to an end a long chapter in the history of humanity's intellectual struggle to understand the universe. But most important of all, *The Zohar* also revolutionizes our consciousness, thereby enhancing the quality of our daily lives.

REVELATION: "OUR ENTRANCE TO THE HIGHER WORLDS . . ."

It is written in *The Zohar*, "All the celestial treasures and hidden mysteries which were not revealed to succeeding generations will be revealed in the Age of Aquarius." It is noted that this new age will provide us with an understanding not only of our familiar universe, but also of that which lies beyond, in the metaphysical domain. Today more than at any other time in history, the Light is demanding to be revealed. As the Light separated those on Mount Sinai from all limitations of the mundane physical world, so shall the Light separate us in the Age of Aquarius!

The Revelation on Mount Sinai is interpreted by *The Zohar* to mean a connection between the raw, naked energy of the Light and humanity. Hence the use of the word "revelation," which means that the Light was disclosed without the usual protective elements that conceal its awesome power. With the removal of the illusory, corporeal realm of existence, the impediments that prevent or slow down our movement cease to exist. At the time of Revelation, the idea of the speed of Light no longer has any reference. Movement is instantaneous once we consciously decide where we want to be. Space as we know it has no place once our illusory, physical realm disappears. Time as we know it flies out the window. Past, future, and present become elevated to unity with the Light.

"The generation of Mount Sinai saw all the future generations of humanity up to the days of the Messiah!" This startling declaration in *The Zohar* reveals that events can operate not only from the past to the future, but also from the future to the past. The Light, therefore, is our time machine, our entrance to the higher worlds. Only the Light is capable of removing the illusion of corporeal reality to reveal a cosmic model that is, was, and will always be timeless and full of certainty.

This was the phenomenon of Revelation. But when Israel fell under the influence of the Golden Calf, Israel's connection with the Light came to an end. The Israelites could no longer harness the awesome power of the Light, and eventually they perished in the wilderness.

Revelation was and is an opportunity to connect with the tools and channels for achieving the altered state of consciousness that enabled Moses to connect with the Light. Once the Light was revealed, there was no turning back. But its power was too much for humanity to handle at that point in time.

Now, at the beginning of the Age of Aquarius, humanity will once again be given the opportunity to connect with the Light. This connection will result in our ability to travel back in time—or, stated another way, to reach and achieve an altered state of consciousness in which the past and future are both now, where our youth is again upon us, and where death has been erased from the landscape of our existence.

If, as *The Zohar* suggests, we are to condition ourselves for the flight back to Mount Sinai when Revelation took place, then in a matter of seconds we will have traveled approximately 3,300 years—faster than the speed of Light. Once we have reached these speeds, science agrees that we can move in reverse time. Having accomplished this feat, we can now become the beneficiaries of all that reverse time has in store for us.

In H. G. Wells' novel *The Time Machine*, a device was built that moved through time but remained in the same physical location. From a scientific point of view, this is not possible even in theory. In the scientist's understanding of time reversal, there must be a change of position as well as a change in time. Time travel means that an object would be transported out of the Light frame into a region that is neither here and now, nor past and future.

At present, the general feeling among cosmologists is that unless some really advanced beings have already made a time machine, we're not going back to visit the dinosaurs. Nonetheless, the issue is here to stay. Richard Feynman once showed that positrons, the antimatter counterparts of electrons, could be regarded as electrons that are moving backward in time. Kabbalists have no difficulty in dealing with this concept. There is a story about the Ari wishing to be in Jerusalem for the

Sabbath. Within minutes, he arrived in Jerusalem from Safed, which is some 200 miles away. There are many stories in *The Zohar* of our sages traveling from one place to another. How is this "miracle" accomplished? What is necessary is a level of transcendence and elevation to the realm of true reality.

How will we achieve this transformation? By Restriction. By transforming our Desire to Receive for Oneself Alone to the Desire to Share. By using all the tools and teachings of Kabbalah.

IN CONCLUSION:
TRANSFORMATION

TRANSFORMATION OF CONSCIOUSNESS

Einstein spent the last 50 years of his life searching for the so-called "theory of everything" that would unite relativity and quantum mechanics, the two revolutionary discoveries of modern physics. Einstein never found what he was looking for. To a kabbalist, this is not surprising—because Einstein was looking in all the wrong places.

The true "theory of everything" lies in the realm of consciousness. Moreover, it is only through a transformation of consciousness that the world will be set free from chaos once and for all.

Everything points toward a consciousness-based reality rather than a physical reality. But some phenomena seem so hard to believe or imagine that even eminent contemporary physicists "hit the wall." Even Einstein, in his middle 70's, succumbed to the perspective of physical experience. He could not accept the fact that common-sense reality was dead.

Through the study of Kabbalah, however, everyone can attain the level of awareness that eluded even the greatest physicist of the 20th century. The principles laid down by *The Zohar* are now accessible to all. We can indeed connect with the world of certainty and order, and leave behind the illusory world of chaos and disorder.

The Zohar leads us to insights of great simplicity and beauty. Its teachings reveal the genuine features of nature. Its wholeness and clarity make us wonder why we hadn't thought about all this before. Its creative imagination produces a theory of reality so compelling in its elegance that we become convinced of its truth even before it is subjected to experimental testing.

This book, like *The Zohar*, is intended to drive home the fact that we have an orderly universe around us. But before we can move ahead and access this universe, we must first rid ourselves of the belief that we are helpless human beings aboard a rudderless ship in a stormy sea. We can and must assure ourselves that we and we alone will master the future course of our life experiences. Life is not a game of chance. Chance is an illusion.

The kabbalist, whose lifestyle includes Restriction in every aspect of daily experience, finds the quantum leap through the barriers of our physical world as easy as crossing a deserted road. When a person is prepared by the teachings of Kabbalah, even time travel is "a piece of cake." Kabbalah restores the mind to a central position in our universe. When we tunnel through space-time and travel at the speed of light toward Revelation and connect with it, we enter the ultimate reality. The Tree of Life universe unfolds itself before our very eyes.

I contend that the thoughts presented here are revolutionary. To be sure, coming to grips with these seemingly outlandish notions does tax the imagination. History has shown us that the truth always turns out to be more wonderful than anything we can imagine. The universe appears to be full of violent activity. To the kabbalist, however, violent phenomena are simply expressions of human violence. Good and evil apply to the Tree of Knowledge universe. However, the kabbalistic journey can prepare us for entrance into the realm of the Tree of Life consciousness, where chaos and disorder will be recognized for what they are: an illusion.

Kabbalah teaches us the way to remove ourselves from the spiritually impoverishing cycle of negativity, struggle, failure, and ultimate defeat. Kabbalah leads us to a state of mind in which we are connected with the infinite continuum—where time, space, and motion are unified; where past, present, and future are entwined; where everyone and everything are interconnected; where then is now, and all is subject to The Power of You.

MORE READING FROM
KABBALIST RAV BERG

TAMING CHAOS

Eminent kabbalist Rav Berg offers a deep, advanced explanation of how the tools of Kabbalah (Ana B'Koach, Kabbalistic Meditation, 72 Names and much more) can be used in everyday life to eliminate chaos.

Chaos is not only pandemonium in the streets and people running around like mad. It is personal chaos. The difficulties that you face each day, from stubbing your toe and getting stuck on long lines to losing money in business, having troubles in relationships and getting sick. Whatever it is that gets in the way of your happiness, this book will show you how to make it work for—not against—you.

THE ESSENTIAL ZOHAR

The Zohar has traditionally been known as the world's most esoteric and profound spiritual document, but kabbalist Rav Berg, this generation's greatest living kabbalist, has dedicated his life to making this wisdom universally available. The vast wisdom and Light of *The Zohar* came into being as a gift to all humanity, and *The Essential Zohar* at last explains this gift to the world.

THE ZOHAR

You've read about the miraculous power of *The Zohar* in the *Power of You*. Now find out how to bring this power into your life.

Composed more than 2,000 years ago, *The Zohar* is a set of 23 books, a commentary on biblical and spiritual matters in the form of conversations among spiritual masters. But to describe *The Zohar* only in physical terms is greatly misleading. In truth, *The Zohar* is nothing less than a powerful tool for achieving the most important purposes of our lives. It was given to all humankind by the Creator to bring us protection, to connect us with the Creator's Light, and ultimately to fulfill our birthright of true spiritual transformation.

Eighty two years ago, when The Kabbalah Centre was founded, *The Zohar* had virtually disappeared from the world. Few people in the general population had ever heard of it. Whoever sought to read it—in any country, in any language, at any price—faced a long and futile search. Today all this has changed. Through the work of The Kabbalah Centre and the editorial efforts of Michael Berg, *The Zohar* is now being brought to the world, not only in the original Aramaic language but also in English.

The new English *Zohar* provides everything for connecting to this sacred text on all levels: the original Aramaic text for scanning; an English translation; and clear, concise commentary for study and learning.

To order your *Zohar*, call our Student Support Department at 1–800–KABBALAH. Our trained instructors are available 18 hours a day to answer any and all of your questions about *The Zohar* and Kabbalah.

This call will change your life forever.

MORE BOOKS THAT CAN HELP YOU BRING THE WISDOM OF KABBALAH INTO YOUR LIFE

THE 72 NAMES OF GOD: TECHNOLOGY FOR THE SOUL™
—a national best-seller by author Yehuda Berg

The story of Moses and the Red Sea is well known to almost everyone; it's even been an Academy Award–winning film. What is not known, according to the internationally prominent author Yehuda Berg, is that a state-of-the-art technology is encoded and concealed within that biblical story. This technology is called the 72 Names of God, and it is the key—your key—to ridding yourself of depression, stress, creative stagnation, anger, illness, and other physical and emotional problems. In fact, the 72 Names of God is the oldest, most powerful tool known to humanity—far more powerful than any 21st century high-tech know-how when it comes to eliminating the garbage in your life so that you can wake up and enjoy life each day. Indeed, the 72 Names of God is the ultimate pill for anything and everything that ails you because it strikes at the DNA level of your soul.

THE POWER OF KABBALAH
—an international best-seller by author Yehuda Berg

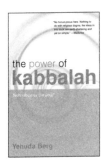

Imagine your life filled with unending joy, purpose, and contentment. Imagine your days infused with pure insight and energy. This is *The Power of Kabbalah*. It is the path from the momentary pleasure that most of us settle for to the lasting fulfillment that is yours to claim. Your deepest desires are waiting to be realized. But they are not limited to the temporary rush you might get from closing a business deal, the short-term high from drugs, or a passionate sexual relationship that lasts for only a few short months.

Wouldn't you like to experience a lasting sense of wholeness and peace that is unshakable, no matter what might be happening around you? Complete fulfillment is the promise of Kabbalah. Within these pages, you will learn how to look at and navigate through life in a whole new way. You will understand your purpose and how to receive the abundant gifts that are waiting for you. By making a critical transformation from a reactive to a proactive being, you will increase your creative energy, gain control of your life, and enjoy new spiritual levels of existence. Kabbalah's ancient teaching is rooted in the perfect union of the physical and spiritual laws already at work in your life. Get ready to experience this exciting realm of awareness, meaning, and joy.

The wonder and wisdom of Kabbalah have influenced the world's leading spiritual, philosophical, religious, and scientific minds. Until today, however, that wisdom was hidden away in ancient texts, available only to scholars who knew where to look. Now, after many centuries, *The Power of Kabbalah* resides in this one remarkable book. Here at long last is the complete and simple path—actions you can take right now to create the life you desire and deserve.

BECOMING LIKE GOD
By Michael Berg

At the age of 16, kabbalistic scholar Michael Berg began the herculean task of translating *The Zohar*, Kabbalah's chief text, from its original Aramaic into its first complete English translation. *The Zohar*, which consists of 23 volumes, is considered a compendium of virtually all information pertaining to the universe, and its wisdom is only beginning to be verified today.

During the ten years he worked on *The Zohar*, Michael Berg discovered the long-lost secret for which humanity has searched for more than 5,000 years: how to achieve our ultimate destiny. *Becoming Like God* reveals the transformative method by which people can actually break free of what is called "ego nature" to achieve total joy and lasting life.

Berg puts forth the revolutionary idea that for the first time in history, an opportunity is being made available to humankind: an opportunity to Become Like God.

THE SECRET
By Michael Berg

Like a jewel that has been painstakingly cut and polished, *The Secret* reveals life's essence in its most concise and powerful form. Michael Berg begins by showing you how our everyday understanding of our purpose in the world is literally backwards. Whenever there is pain in our lives—indeed, whenever there is anything less than complete joy and fulfillment—this basic misunderstanding is the reason.

As the book continues, you will be introduced to stories and insights from the greatest sages of Kabbalah. You will learn how you can free yourself from unhappiness and gain the joy and fulfillment that is your true destiny. *The Secret* is a book that will open your eyes, touch your heart, and change your life forever!

AUDIO RESOURCES

THE POWER OF KABBALAH AUDIO SERIES

The Power of Kabbalah is nothing less than a user's guide to the universe. Move beyond where you are right now to where you truly want to be—emotionally, spiritually, and creatively. This exciting audio series brings you the ancient, authentic teaching of Kabbalah in a powerful, practical audio format.

CREATING MIRACLES IN YOUR LIFE

We're used to thinking of a miracle as something that happens at the whim of God. But the kabbalists have long taught that the true power to create miracles is present in each and every one of us—if only we can learn to access that power and put it into practice. This inspiring tape series shows how to do exactly that. Order it now, and enter the zone of the miraculous!

TRUE PROSPERITY

True Prosperity is an entirely new paradigm for achieving total financial fulfillment. It provides a simple set of concepts and tools to remove the fundamental spiritual blocks that prevent prosperity from materializing in all areas of your life.

This unique program teaches kabbalistic concepts and tools that can be specifically applied to the world of business and money. When you know the spiritual laws of money, you'll never have to worry about money again.

THE KABBALAH CENTRE

THE INTERNATIONAL LEADER
IN THE EDUCATION OF KABBALAH

Since its founding, The Kabbalah Centre has had a single mission: to improve and transform people's lives by bringing the power and wisdom of Kabbalah to all who wish to partake of it.

Through the lifelong efforts of Rav Berg, his wife Karen, and the great spiritual lineage of which they are a part, an astonishing 3.5 million people around the world have already been touched by the powerful teachings of Kabbalah. And each year, the numbers are growing!

As the leading source of kabbalistic wisdom with 50 locations around the world, The Kabbalah Centre offers you a wealth of resources, including:

- The English *Zohar*, the first-ever comprehensive English translation of the foundation of kabbalistic wisdom. In 23 beautifully bound volumes, this edition includes the full Aramaic text, the English translation, and detailed commentary, making this once-inaccessible text understandable to all.

- A full schedule of workshops, lectures, and evening classes for students at all levels of knowledge and experience.

- CDs, audiotapes and videotapes, and books in English and ten other languages.

- One of the Internet's most exciting and comprehensive websites, **www.kabbalah.com**—which receives more than 100,000 visitors each month.

- A constantly expanding list of events and publications to help you live *The Secret* and other teachings of Kabbalah with greater understanding and excitement.

Discover why The Kabbalah Centre is one of the world's fastest-growing spiritual organizations. Our sole purpose is to improve people's lives through the teachings of Kabbalah. Let us show you what Kabbalah can do for you!

Each Kabbalah Centre location hosts free introductory lectures. For more information on Kabbalah or on these and other products and services, call 1-800-KABBALAH.

Wherever you are, there's a Kabbalah Centre—because now you can call 1-800-KABBALAH from almost anywhere, 18 hours a day, and get answers or guidance right over the telephone. You'll be connected to distinguished senior faculty who are on hand to help you understand Kabbalah as deeply as you want to—whether it involves recommending a course of study; deciding which books/tapes to take or the order in which to take them; discussing the material; or anything else you wish to know about Kabbalah.